Acknowledgments

I am grateful for all those who, through God's grace, have entered my life and provided care for my soul during the creation of *Heart to Heart*. Many women, and a few good men, gave counsel, shared their own growth experiences, and encouraged me to keep going. I gratefully acknowledge the commitment of my heart-centered assistant, Margaret Carter, who believed in me, added the personal contact with the trial groups, and kept me organized.

I also wish to express my appreciation to my friends and colleagues Adele Wilcox and Betty Sohm Johnson, who read many drafts, offering clear-headed advice and doses of humor as needed. Special mention must be made of Sara Martz, Cathie McFadden, Lucy Wray, Linda Hetrick, and Arlene Brown (my mom), who used the materials with women's groups and gave me generous feedback that contributed to making this resource true to life and down to earth. Thanks also to Nita Bean for her encouragement and design ideas and to Joan Marie Laflamme for her initial editing work, which sharpened my communication. Of course, this resource would not be a reality without my friends at Dimensions for Living and my excellent colleague and editor, Sally Sharpe.

To my husband, Dale, for his patience; to my son Stephen, for his kisses; and to my eldest son, Christian, for his computer assistance, go big hugs. To my "bosses," David Brewer and James Jennings; my colleagues, spiritual support groups, and friends of the Florida Conference of The United Methodist Church; and most of all, to the Gracious Source of my creativity and delight, the God who knows me yet still puts up with me, I offer forever my gratitude.

D1304714

5

Introduction

"It doesn't get better than this," I say to my friend as we sit at her kitchen counter. In fact, the conversation has been so replete with genuine care, down-to-earth "mother wisdom," and humor that I am reluctant to abandon my now empty coffee mug and leave.

"Why can't we take more time to do just this?" I ask. The *we* refers to friends, colleagues, and women I'd like to know but am always too busy to spend time with. The *we* extends to all women who need a place where they may share concerns—some sensitive, some thorny. And so, *Heart to Heart* was born.

What is Heart to Heart?

We women often come together in a hive of activity for worthwhile causes. Congregations are swarming with such activities. Yet, rarely do we slow long enough with one another to find the deep-seated spirit of renewal we desperately long for. *Heart to Heart* is an innovative program that changes the ways we get together as women. It is a response to the multitude of us who seek a deeper spirituality in Christ—many of whom, for years, deny and repress what we know is true: We need to take time to nourish our own lives even as we give to others. When we don't take the time necessary for prayer, study, meditation, solitude, and caring for our physical selves, we consequently live in contradictions, inviting internal conflict. Our lives take on a frantic quality. But as we turn our hearts to God, we experience deep within ourselves a reorientation of values that tell us we are worthy of God's care and love.

The title, *Heart to Heart*, comes from the Christian tradition that sees the heart not only as a physical part of the body but also as the center of the person, drawing together mind, body, and spirit. One ancient Christian teacher, Theophan the Recluse, tells us: "Find a place in your heart and speak there with the Lord. It is the Lord's reception room."

Heart to Heart speaks to the heart, which extends inward to God and outward to family and community.

Heart to Heart is a spiritual growth group designed to help you, and a group of women gathering with you, seek and hear God's will for your lives as you grow in friendship together. While *Heart to Heart* is written for women of the Christian faith, women seeking faith also will find meaning and enlightenment in the experience. This innovative spiritual journey will lead you through an experience of peer ministry, self-discovery, mutual encouragement, prayer, and Bible study. Although *Heart to Heart* is not primarily a Bible study group, Sacred Scripture and Christ-centered teachings are at its core. (For more on the role of Bible study in *Heart to Heart*, see pages 42–45.) Together you will strive to create an environment of camaraderie and support, both intellectual and spiritual. Not only will you experience the lessons of each gathering but you also will tell your own stories and bond as each of you gains insight into your place in the world. As a result, you will discover important "pieces" that often are missing from your lives: hospitality and genuine community.

The purpose of *Heart to Heart*, then, is to lead you and the women gathering with you to greater self-awareness and awaken you to God's Spirit in your lives, while teaching you new ways to inspire, encourage, and affirm one another. Through the process of spiritual growth, you will clarify your values as centered in Christ (the nonnegotiable belief system you base your life on); claim your own giftedness, which has been given to you by the Holy Spirit; and return these new strengths of faith to your family relationships and to the larger community.

How does Heart to Heart "work"?

The *Heart to Heart* program is a twelve-session journey that allows groups of all sizes—from just a few to one hundred or more—to meet weekly or monthly according to their schedules and needs. This is explained in detail on pages 20–21.

Heart to Heart is designed so that your group may have the option of a thirty- or sixty-minute gathering. Decide which time length best suits your group members' needs and schedules. Groups tend to fill the time they have, leaving important matters until last, regardless how much time is allotted. A great deal can be accomplished in thirty minutes or in sixty minutes. Whatever you decide, your group should stick strictly to the time schedule at every gathering. Maintaining the schedule allows everyone to be present for the full gathering. Remember, there are always exceptions.

The sixty-minute option includes Sacred Story Bible Study as part of every gathering, making this an excellent choice for small group ministries as well as the Sunday school program of a congregation. The thirty-minute option allows participants to use the Bible study as part of their ongoing journal work outside of the group's time together. The shorter gathering is an excellent format for already-established women's circles, as well as Bible study and mission groups wanting to attract a new or younger constituency. Such groups, which generally meet for a full hour, may follow the thirty-minute *Heart to Heart* gathering with their usual programming or business meeting.

Perhaps one of the most attractive features of *Heart to Heart* is that it does not follow a traditional teacher-student approach. Instead, it relies heavily upon shared leadership and group interaction. The materials are ready for your group to gather and use. There is no lesson preparation required for participants.

Rather than a group leader or teacher, your *Heart to Heart* group will need a group coordinator. This person organizes and facilitates the introductory session (see pages 33–41); acquires the resources and materials needed for each gathering; creates a supply box; or delegates these tasks (see pages 180–83 for a list of needed supplies and equipment). The coordinator also coordinates the weekly or monthly gatherings. (See "Frequently Asked Questions," pages 13–24, for more details.)

Every gathering will follow the same basic format, with occasional variations in the order of Bible study:

- **Circle of Hearts**—a time to gather and greet one another
- **Heartwarmers**—an opening ritual including guided prayer and breathing exercises
- **A Heart-Centered Story**—a continuing story about the woman in search of her heart
- **Sacred Story Bible Study**—a creative approach to Bible study. (*Note: If your group chooses the thirty-minute option, you will skip this por-*

tion of the gathering and use the Bible study as part of your ongoing journal work during the week.)

- **From the Heart Journal: A Personal Prayer Journal for Women—** time for journaling in your personal journals
- **A Hearty Goodbye—**a closing exercise

Other activities appearing at various times and in various gatherings include **Heartbeat**—opportunities for using suggested music—and **You've Got to Have Heart**—special times for sharing with one another.

What else do I need to know about Heart to Heart?

With this introduction, turn next to "Frequently Asked Questions" (pages 13–24) for more information about *Heart to Heart.* In addition to some new details, you will find much of the information contained in this introduction repeated there in a format designed to be reproduced and shared with women in an introductory session of *Heart to Heart.* Then, continue reading through the materials in Part 1, which are provided to familiarize you with the program and prepare you for what lies ahead.

As you begin this exciting journey, pause now to make a commitment to prayer. This prayer should center on a constant awareness of the holy within yourself and within each woman you encounter. A significant outcome of the *Heart to Heart* experience is the affirmation that each woman is indeed a holy child of God and important in God's divine plan. Each woman is the beloved of God. Every woman in your *Heart to Heart* group will experience heartfelt care, because *Heart to Heart* is about a woman's heart being *centered in God's love.* Pray, then, that as you gather together, the Holy Spirit will be at work, bringing clarity about God's will for your lives and a deepened spirituality.

Part 1

Getting Acquainted
with
Heart to Heart

Frequently Asked Questions

What is Heart to Heart all about?

*H*eart to Heart is a spiritual growth group designed to help you and a group of women gathering with you seek and hear God's will for your lives as you grow in friendship together. It is not primarily a Bible study, although Sacred Scripture and Christ-centered teachings are at its core. Although the program is written for women of the Christian faith, women who are seeking faith also will find meaning and enlightenment in the experience.

The purpose of *Heart to Heart* is to lead you to greater self-awareness and awaken you to God's Spirit in your lives while teaching you new ways to inspire, encourage, and affirm one another. *Heart to Heart*, then, is an innovative and gentle program designed to help you grow spiritually. Through this process of spiritual growth, you will clarify your values—the nonnegotiable belief system you base your life on—claim your own gifts, and return these new strengths to your family relationships and to the larger community.

What will I experience?

Heart to Heart is a series of twelve gatherings that will lead you and the women in your group through an experience of peer ministry, self-discovery, mutual support, prayer, and Bible study. It combines creative energy, mother-wisdom (passed across generations from woman to woman), and "sister spirit" (the unique fellowship of women) to foster a sense of belonging, hospitality, faith-sharing, and genuine community.

Together you will strive to create an environment of camaraderie and support, both intellectual and spiritual. Not only will you experience the lessons of each gathering but you also will tell your own stories and bond as each of you gains insight into your place in the world. The gatherings will validate your concerns and questions about life, love, God, family, and community, and will offer the opportunity for "venting" when needed. You also will have lots of chances to enjoy lighthearted laughter!

Who may come to Heart to Heart?

Heart to Heart participants are women who are looking for a "new word" in spiritual growth. The program sidesteps "churchy" language, which no longer appeals to many people, and provides a comfortable way for women of faith to build and nurture relationships with one another—much in the way the popular "girlfriend" movement has done in secular society through women's reading groups in recent years.

All women are welcome to be part of *Heart to Heart*. It is good for women to set aside specific times in their hectic schedules to pause and consider their lives. For this reason, *Heart to Heart* encompasses women of all ages, from late teens to senior citizens. The experience appeals especially to women who are in their twenties to forties.

May I invite my friends?

Yes! *Heart to Heart* may serve as an "evangelistic port of entry" to ease new women into the congregation's larger fellowship. Informal neighborhood groups of women also will feel "at home" because of its core spiritual teachings and ecumenical nature. The program has been designed in such a way as to discourage cliques and make newcomers feel welcome.

Keep in mind that your group is not an elite women's club, excluding others. You are a part of the body of Christ. A core mission of your group may be to reach out to other women to share what you are discovering about God and the worthiness of your own lives. The women's Christian spirituality group model, upon which *Heart to Heart* is based, is one of sharing—talents, blessings, and works—so that the community may be a place of healing and transformation for all women.

Welcoming new women into the experience of care and growth is essential to the identity and health of any women's group. Your group will want to continually look for ways to extend yourselves to all women.

Who leads the group?

There is no designated teacher or leader. Just as women gather in a kitchen to prepare a meal, form teams at their place of employment to work on a project, or volunteer to accomplish a task, the women in your group will work together as a whole. As you take turns guiding the group through the gathering, according to the easy-to-follow instructions provided in the *Guidebook*, each of you will be able to do your part in a way that fits who you are.

Rather than a teacher or leader, your group will need a group coordinator. This person organizes and facilitates the introductory session; acquires the resources and materials needed for each gathering; creates a supply box; or delegates these tasks; and coordinates the weekly or monthly gatherings. Although the group coordinator is responsible for room setup prior to the introductory session, this task is shared by all group members for gatherings 1–12. The supply box may be kept in the gathering room so that the women may access it quickly and conveniently at the beginning of each gathering. If using the multiple groups format, one or more supply boxes may be stored in a central location so that various groups may pick up their supplies prior to each gathering.

Remember, the primary role of the group coordinator is to handle organizational matters, not to teach or lead the group. No special training or "credentials" are required!

What happens at the gatherings?

Each gathering includes the following:
- Prayer rituals that will help you find your identity in Christ.
- "The Quest of the Woman in Search of Her Heart," a continuing story in which you will identify your own concerns and cares and come to see more clearly who you are and where you are going.
- Sacred Story Bible Study, an effective way to study the Bible using four different methods that will move you and dramatically impact your life.
- Down-to-earth practices that will help you deepen your spiritual experience in everyday life, such as using relaxation exercises, praying, claiming quiet times, and journaling.
- Opportunities for sharing with the other women in your group.
- Music to soothe the soul.

How is music used in the gatherings?

Inspirational music provides a soulful gateway to spiritual feelings and ideas. The power of music is a gift from above that brings together the sacred and the sensual. Music carries us beyond the everyday to embody something greater than ourselves. It connects the earthly and the divine.

Music is an important part of the *Heart to Heart* experience. You will find suggestions of when and how to use specific kinds of music during the gatherings in the materials included in Part 2 of the *Guidebook*. For example, you are encouraged to play soothing meditative music as a respite from the hectic pace of ordinary life as you gather and greet one another. You also will discover that playing gentle music in the background at various times during your gatherings will make the women in your group feel "at home," help ease you into silences, and cover up distracting noise. When choosing music for times of silent reflection, you will want to stay away from familiar songs whose lyrics may distract the thoughts of participants. At other times during your gatherings music that invites singing or stirring, energized movement will be suggested.

Whatever style of music you decide to use at various times during your gatherings, you will discover that the music will help carry you to symbolic realms of contemplation and communion with God that elude your grasp in any other way. The music is not an end in itself, but a vehicle for the renewal of your heart in worship to God.

How much time do the gatherings take?

Heart to Heart is designed so that your group may have the option of a thirty- or sixty-minute gathering. The sixty-minute option includes Bible study as part of every gathering. The thirty-minute option allows participants to use the Bible study as part of their ongoing journal work outside of the group's time together. Decide which option best suits your group members' needs and schedules. Whatever you decide, your group should stick strictly to the time scheduled at every gathering. Beginning and ending on time allows everyone to be present for the full gathering. Remember, however, that there are always exceptions.

How much time will it take me to prepare for a gathering?

There is no preparation time for participants and limited preparation time for the group coordinator, especially if she delegates some tasks. *Heart to Heart* acknowledges your busy schedules. Each of you attends as a guest. As the gathering begins, open your *Guidebook* to the appropriate gathering and begin, allowing the material to lead you step-by-step through the experience.

What will I need to bring with me?

Every woman participating in *Heart to Heart* will need two resources: *Heart to Heart Guidebook: A Spiritual Journey for Women*, and *From the Heart Journal: A Personal Prayer Journal for Women*. You will need to bring these with you to each gathering. Because all of the

Bible passages to be studied are printed in your journal, you will not need to bring a Bible. (Note: *Heart to Heart* uses the New Revised Standard Version of the Bible. If your group prefers another translation, you may bring Bibles with you.)

Why is journaling a part of Heart to Heart?

Journaling is another important component of the *Heart to Heart* experience. Your journaling will bring greater clarity to your relationships with God, yourself, and others. It will help you explore some of the everyday dynamics of following Christ: self-acceptance, spirituality, feelings, personal growth, and friendships. Your guided prayer journal, *From the Heart Journal: A Personal Prayer Journal for Women*, will aid you in reflecting on your own experiences, help you to realize the sacredness of your call or "mission" in life, and prepare you to share your story with the group. However, you are free to share—or not to share—from your journal as you choose.

You will be directed to most of the journaling activities as you go through the gatherings. Some additional journal activities are included for you to use as you like.

Do I have to share my feelings all the time?

Any time you do not wish to talk when it is your turn to share during a gathering, simply say, "Pass." At all times you are free to share exactly to the extent you choose. *Heart to Heart* also encourages the practice of active, compassionate listening. Often we feel we must respond to everything that is said. During your first gathering, you and the other women in your group will pray together, asking for the wisdom to know when to speak and when to be silent. Sometimes it will be appropriate for you to respond to others in your group verbally; at other times listening will be the best response. Don't be afraid of silence. Learn to accept what others share as a gift. As you allow one another to share freely and learn to refrain from responding when it is unnecessary or unhelpful, you will experience what it means to serve as the compassionate presence of Christ to one another.

What kind of Bible study will we be doing?

Heart to Heart includes Sacred Story Bible Study, which uses four Bible study methods to explore Jesus and the women in his life and his parables. As you interact with these biblical stories, following the step-by-step directions of each method, not only will you experience the lessons they offer, you also will naturally be led to tell your own story and to bond with the others in your group as you gain insight into your place in the world.

When we tell our stories alongside the gospel story, we become more aware of how God is speaking to us. When we listen carefully with our hearts as well as our heads, God's Word touches us in greater ways than we ever imagined possible.

May Heart to Heart be used with existing Bible study groups and other women's groups?

The thirty-minute option, which does not include Bible study as part of the gathering, is an excellent format for already established women's circles as well as Bible study and mission groups wanting to attract a new or younger constituency. Such groups, which generally meet for a full hour, may follow the thirty-minute *Heart to Heart* gathering with their usual programming or business meeting. The sixty-minute option, which includes Sacred Story Bible Study as part of every gathering, is an excellent choice for small group ministries as well as the Sunday school program of a congregation.

How are gatherings scheduled?

Groups may choose to meet weekly or monthly according to their schedules and needs. It is recommended that your group agree upon a regular meeting time and place. If, however, you have a large number of women who are interested in participating (as often is the case in large churches or in ecumenical efforts sponsored by various community churches), and if some of you find it difficult to work another regular meeting date into an already packed and continually changing schedule, you might consider the *multiple groups format.* This is similar to the meeting plans used so successfully by support groups such as Weight Watchers and Alcoholics Anonymous. Here is how it works. Plan a schedule of multiple *Heart to Heart* gatherings each week or month, all using the same material (or session) from the *Guidebook.* Each participant plugs into the gathering that best suits her schedule for a given week or month. For example, if a woman has a dental appointment on Tuesday morning, when one gathering is scheduled, she may attend another gathering during the week—morning, afternoon, or evening; in a home, at the church, or in another designated meeting place. (Whenever three or more are able to meet, a gathering may be scheduled.)

The multiple groups format not only accommodates busy women's schedules but also keeps groups from growing cliquish and encourages open membership. Again, this arrangement works particularly well in large congregations.

If we choose the multiple groups format, how do we keep track of one another?

Because various groups of women are meeting at different times, using attendance cards or sign-in sheets is extremely helpful. The cards or sheets should be kept in an envelope and stored with the other materials needed for the gathering. Each woman marks the sign-in sheet or her attendance card before the meeting begins. You may designate a person to check all the attendance cards of the various groups and follow up with women who have missed more than two gatherings. This task also may be shared by volunteers.

Where do we meet?

You can meet anywhere—a church, a home, a restaurant, a community center, in the meeting room at the library, and so forth.

What kind of room and equipment do we need?

You will need a room that is large enough for you to meet as a full group as well as break into smaller groups of three to five. Arrange comfortable chairs in a large circle, and place a small table—to be used as a focus center—in the center of the circle. (See pages 29–31 for information on how to create a focus center.)

You'll need a tape or CD player and warm, welcoming music to play as you gather, as well as other musical selections to play at various times during your gatherings. (See "Bibliography of Suggested Music" on pages 200–03.)

If possible, dim the overhead lighting or use lamps to achieve the maximum effect from the lighted candle on the focus center and to give the room a more intimate atmosphere. (See pages 29–31 for more details about room setup and equipment.)

How do we keep time?

You may find it helps to have a watch or clock at all of your gatherings. Sometimes you will move apart to engage in individual reflection and writing. Other times you will divide into small groups. A specific amount of time is allocated for such activities. Take turns keeping time. Ringing a bell—which may be placed on the focus center—is an easy way to call everyone back together when "time is up."

What is the expected dress?

Come as you are. Wear everyday clothes. Jeans or work-out gear is fine, as is a business suit. As *Heart to Heart* women, you will meet in relaxed ways to share stories, sort out your lives, and reassess God's will for yourselves.

21

What about children?

Children are always welcome. Their interruptions are viewed as part of the weave of the gathering. Be sure to "childproof" the location. Your group may designate a particular gathering at which children are especially welcome or at which childcare is provided—or you may choose to provide childcare at every gathering. Some groups find a volunteer to care for the children at the site or in her own home. Another option is to collect dues to pay for a caretaker if the group prefers childcare outside of the gathering. Share any expense. Whatever arrangements are made, remember that childcare is the responsibility of the entire community. If children are considered, mothers with children will attend.

What about food?

The decision to have food or not to have food at your gatherings is entirely up to you. It is recommended, however, that you consider not serving food in order to eliminate the burden of food preparation. Some women in your group may make arrangements to go out for coffee or a meal afterward; this is neither encouraged nor discouraged. Of course, if your group is using *Heart to Heart* for a full evening or a weekend "retreat," you probably will want to serve some good, healthy food to boost energy levels.

Why use nametags?

Nametags help women learn one another's names quickly. Even if the women in your group know one another, nametags indicate that you are not a clique but an open group; a new person may join you at any time. For groups choosing the multiple groups format, nametags enable each woman to attend the meeting that best suits her schedule without feeling alienated because she does not know some or all of the other participants. (Note: Because the nametags are used over and over at each gathering, use nametag holders made of sturdy plastic or other durable material. Nametag inserts that may be reproduced, cut apart, and slipped inside the holders are provided on page 191.)

What if I miss some of the gatherings?

Women who miss gatherings, no matter what the reason or how many times they miss, always are welcomed back. We all have times

in our lives when, for whatever reason, we cannot be somewhere we're supposed to be. We need to remember to respect the ebb and flow of one another's life and accept that we are at different places.

What happens when we've finished Heart to Heart?

Many *Heart to Heart* groups want to continue meeting after the initial twelve gatherings. For information about other resources your *Heart to Heart* group might like to use, see "Bibliography of Recommended Resources" in the Appendix, pages 204–05.

Overview of the Gatherings

*ach Heart to Heart gathering follows a basic format, although there are occasional differences. A consistent difference between groups meeting for sixty minutes and groups meeting for thirty minutes is the use of Sacred Story Bible Study. Sixty-minute groups include the Bible study as part of every gathering. Thirty-minute groups skip this portion of the gathering and use the Bible study as part of their ongoing journal work outside of their time together.

A typical sixty-minute *Heart to Heart* gathering includes the following:

Circle of Hearts

Greet one another and follow the instructions in the *Guidebook* to get started.

Heartwarmers

Next, the *Guidebook* leads you through an opening prayer ritual. After lighting the Christ candle on the focus center, you may pray together, share a brief Scripture reading, sing a song, and so forth. Relaxed breathing and guided prayer exercises also help you make the shift to a more responsive attitude.

A Heart-Centered Story

Each gathering includes a segment of a continuing story, "The Quest of the Woman in Search of Her Heart." Through her journey, you find your way back to your own heart.

Sacred Story Bible Study

At each gathering, you use one of four methods of Sacred Story Bible Study to study Jesus and the women in his life and his parables. Each Sacred Story holds a special lesson for the heart. (Note: The order in which the Bible study comes during the gathering varies from gathering to gathering. In some, it follows journaling time; in others, it precedes journaling. If your group is meeting for thirty minutes, skip this portion of the gathering and use the Bible study as part of your ongoing journal work at home.)

From the Heart Journal: A Personal Prayer Journal for Women

Each of you spends some time in silent reflection as you write in your journal. This thought-provoking guided journal helps you clarify your values as centered in Christ and helps you share your reflections with others.

A Hearty Goodbye

Closing prayer rituals remind you who you are and "whose" you are. Thus prepared, you may reenter the world renewed. At this time the group shares a prayer, Scripture verse, poem, symbols, or reflective words. After discussing the date, time, and place for your next gathering, you depart with a word of blessing.

Other activities appearing at various times and in various gatherings include "Heartbeat"—opportunities for using suggested music—and "You've Got to Have Heart"—special times for sharing with one another.

Remember, each group is unique. Let your gatherings be a reflection of the special women who have come together. Some *Heart to Heart* groups add more music or prayers. Others find a ritual that is special to them and repeat it at each gathering. Still other groups use more visual imagery or decorate their focus centers in colorful, artistic ways. In other words, don't be afraid to veer away from the *Guidebook* plan. God's Spirit is creative!

Getting Started

The First Step

*H*ere are two ways you may get *Heart to Heart* off and running. The first, the "Quick-Start Method," works well for small groups and existing groups of women interested in using *Heart to Heart*.

Quick-Start Method
1. Gather together at least three women.
2. Set a time and place for your gatherings.
3. Acquire the resources and needed materials (see "Equipment and Supplies Checklist," pages 180–83).
4. Begin. (Note: To familiarize everyone in your group with the *Heart to Heart* program and the format of the gatherings, you might want to begin with the introductory session found on pages 33–41. This will extend the total number of gatherings to thirteen. If this is not possible, encourage all participants to read through Part 1 of the *Guidebook* prior to your first gathering. You also will want to distribute and review copies of the "Be-Attitudes," page 187, at your first gathering.)

A second method, which also offers an introductory session, is used primarily by congregations and organizations desiring to introduce a large number of women to *Heart to Heart*, so that they may decide if they want to be involved. The introductory session also allows you to collect the information necessary for organizing groups and, if you choose, setting up the multiple groups format (see pages 20–21 for more details).

Introductory Session Start-Up Method

1. Announce and publicize your introductory session. (See the Appendix, pages 193–97, for a variety of materials to help you announce and publicize your introductory session. Feel free to adapt the materials to suit your particular situation.)
2. Prepare for and facilitate the introductory session (see "Introductory Session," pages 33–41).
3. Organize interested participants into groups. If choosing the multiple groups format, use the sample registration and attendance cards in the Appendix (page 192) to obtain the information needed for creating a schedule of multiple gathering dates and times.
4. Solicit a group coordinator for each group.
5. Provide instructions or assistance to group coordinators for acquiring the resources and needed materials for their groups (see page 180–83ß).

Room Setup and "Atmosphere" for Heart to Heart Gatherings

Plan to meet in an area where there will be few interruptions. The room should be large enough for the women to meet as a full group as well as break into smaller groups of three to five.

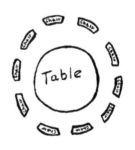

You will want to create an appealing environment in your gathering room. The ideal room setup consists of comfortable chairs arranged in a circle. Create an attractive "focus center" inside the circle to remind you why you have come: so that God's Spirit will live more fully in all. First, drape a small table with a tablecloth or piece of fabric. If you like, you may add an attractive scarf for a personal touch. Then place a candle on the table as a reminder of the Holy Spirit's presence (use a quality pillar candle in an attractive holder or a large "glass jar candle" with a removable lid). You may choose other symbols of the heart for your table to help the

women in your group "center" during your time together. You also will want to have the following items on the table: matches or a lighter; permanent nametags and a wide-edged felt-tip marker; a hand-sized heart made of glass, wood, or other material (to pass around the circle when sharing); a heart-shaped "box"—with removable lid—made of glass, cardboard, or wood (to serve as a heart symbol and to use in various activities); and a bell (to call the group back together after quiet journaling time). (Read on for more details about equipment and supplies.)

Lighting is another effective way to create an inviting atmosphere. If possible, dim the overhead lighting or use lamps to achieve the maximum effect from the lighted candle on the focus center and to make the room more intimate.

Music also will help to "set the mood" throughout your gatherings. Inspirational music provides a soulful gateway to spiritual feelings and ideas. The power of music is a gift from above that brings together the sacred and the sensual. Music carries us beyond the everyday to embody something greater than ourselves. It connects the earthly and the divine. Playing gentle music in the background at certain times during your gatherings will make everyone in your group feel "at home," help ease you into silences, and cover up distracting noise. As you gather, use soothing meditative music as a respite from the hectic pace of ordinary life. Have someone play soothing songs on a piano, guitar, or other instrument, or play selected recordings on a CD or tape player. Remember to play the music again at the end of the gathering as you visit and prepare to leave.

Music is suggested at other times during your gatherings, such as times of silent reflection and times inviting singing or energized movement. Simply follow the music cues, called "Heartbeat," appearing throughout Part 2 of the *Guidebook*, allowing your group to determine other times and ways music can be most effective in your group. (A "Bibliography of Suggested Music" is provided in the Appendix. See pages 200–03.) When choosing music for times of silent reflection, it is recommended that you stay away from songs with familiar tunes or lyrics that may distract your thoughts. Whatever style of music you decide to use at various times during your gatherings, it will help carry you to symbolic realms of contemplation and communion with God that elude your grasp in any other way. The music is not an end in itself, but a vehicle for the renewal of your hearts in worship to God.

Equipment and Supplies

Just as ingredients combine to make a recipe, so *Heart to Heart* is enhanced by the materials used to create the atmosphere, set the mood, and carry out the various exercises and activities. All of the suggested equipment and supplies may be easily and inexpensively obtained. You should be able to purchase everything your group needs—other than books—for roughly forty to fifty dollars. That's only three to four dollars per gathering! Remember, the group coordinator should acquire the materials for your group—or delegate this task to one or more persons. Complete lists of equipment and supplies needed for each gathering are included in the Appendix (see pages 180–83). Feel free to make adjustments and substitutions to these lists as necessary. Just as no two women participating in *Heart to Heart* are exactly alike, so also groups may personalize their gatherings with the materials they choose.

The group coordinator may choose to purchase the materials needed for all twelve gatherings before the first gathering, or, if she prefers, she may purchase materials as needed prior to each gathering. In either case, she will find it helps to place the items in a lightweight box or other container to create a supply box. If you like, your group may decorate the supply box in some way. Cover it with wrapping paper or pictures from magazines. Get out your paints and go crazy. Use your imagination! You will want to store your supply box in your gathering room or another easily accessible location. If using the multiple groups format, one or more supply boxes may be stored in a central location for access by various groups.

Before each gathering...

The group coordinator may find the following checklist helpful when coordinating each gathering:
- Contact all participants and remind them of the date, time, and place

for the gathering. (Note: After announcing the first gathering, you may do this verbally at the end of every gathering. If your church or organization is using the multiple groups format, distribute a printed schedule of all *Heart to Heart* gatherings. Be sure that you—or the person or persons designated to the task—check the attendance cards or sign-in sheet and follow up with those women who have missed more than two gatherings.)

- Review the list of equipment and supplies needed for the gathering (see pages 180–83); secure all materials and place them in a box or other container that may be conveniently stored and retrieved at the beginning of the gathering. (Note: This task may be delegated or shared by several women.) If purchasing all supplies prior to Gathering 1, check the supply box prior to each gathering to ensure that all is in order. Be sure not to forget a CD or tape player and appropriate musical selections for the gathering.
- Although room setup is a shared responsibility for gatherings 1 through 12, including the arrangement of the focus center, you may want to take the initiative in attending to lighting, music, and other important details.

Introductory
Session

Materials Needed

For this session you will need the following items:

- focus center
  —table
  —tablecloth, fabric, and/or attractive scarf
  —pillar candle in attractive holder or large "glass jar candle" with removable lid
  —matches or lighter
  —heart symbols *(optional)*
- music *(instrumentalist or recorded music and the means to play it)*
- nametags *(Note: Stick-on nametags are fine for the introductory session only.)*
- wide-edged felt-tip marker
- newsprint
- books *(one copy of each)*
  —*Heart to Heart Guidebook: A Spiritual Journey for Women*
  —*From the Heart Journal: A Personal Prayer Journal for Women*
- pencils or pens *(one for each woman)*
- refreshments *(e.g., cookies, fruit, beverages)*
- registration/attendance cards, page 192 *(one for each woman; see instructions provided)*
- "Be-Attitudes," page 187 *(one for each woman)*
- "Opening Hearts Sacred Story Bible Study: Great Is Your Faith! (Introductory Session)", pages 188–90 *(one for each woman; duplicate on front and back of one sheet of colored paper)*

Step-by-Step Presentation

Welcome

> Welcome the women as they arrive. Use nametags for those attending. Print names in **BIG BOLD LETTERS.** Provide refreshments such as cookies, fruit, and beverages to show hospitality as the women arrive, or serve refreshments at the end of the meeting as people visit. After the group gathers, stand in front and extend a welcome. If you like, you may ask several women to share in the presentation. The following "script" may help you. Adapt it for your particular situation. Put it in your own words. Don't just read it!

Welcome to this introductory session of *Heart to Heart*. In the first half-hour we will tell you about *Heart to Heart* and answer your questions. During the second half-hour, you will experience a small part of a typical *Heart to Heart* gathering.

A Short Introduction

First, let me tell you about *Heart to Heart*.

> Hold up copies of *Heart to Heart Guidebook: A Spiritual Journey for* Women, and *From the Heart Journal: A Personal Prayer Journal for Women.*

Heart to Heart is the name given to an innovative program designed to help women grow spiritually. Conceived over coffee in a friend's kitchen, it is now being used by women across the country. As a gentle program focusing on the spirituality of women, *Heart to Heart* successfully brings about a sense of belonging and an experience of faith-sharing to the women who participate.

The purpose of *Heart to Heart* is to lead us to greater self-awareness and to awaken us to God's Spirit in our lives, while teaching us new ways to inspire, encourage, and affirm one another.

> Hold up *From the Heart Journal: A Personal Prayer Journal for Women* again.

This personal prayer journal, *From the Heart Journal*, will help guide each of us through this process of personal and spiritual growth.

A Brief Time of Sharing

Each of you now will have two minutes to share. Turn to a woman sitting beside you, introduce yourself, and ask: "Why have you come today? What do you hope to find in *Heart to Heart?*" I will let you know when two minutes are up so that you may switch your roles of talker and listener.

> Keep time. Let the group know when two minutes have elapsed and remind them to switch roles. After another two minutes have passed, continue.

An Overview of Heart to Heart

Heart to Heart is a twelve-session journey that will lead us through an experience of peer ministry, self-discovery, mutual support, Bible study, and prayer. As we share our stories and bond, each of us will gain insights into our current mission in the world. We also will experience two important elements missing from many of our lives: hospitality and genuine community. Each of us will have the opportunity to clarify our values as centered in Christ, claim our own giftedness, and return these new strengths to our family relationships and to the larger community.

Pass out copies of *Heart to Heart* Overview, page 186.

Each *Heart to Heart* group meets weekly or monthly, as group members prefer, for a total of twelve gatherings. The step-by-step "blueprint" for each gathering is included in the *Guidebook*.

Hold up a copy of the *Guidebook*.

Because there is no preparation time for participants and only limited preparation for the group coordinator—the person responsible for securing supplies and coordinating the gatherings—and because *Heart to Heart* uses shared leadership rather than one designated teacher or leader, the group simply gathers and begins, following the instructions provided in the *Guidebook*.

Heart to Heart is designed so that each group may have the option of a thirty- or sixty-minute gathering. The sixty-minute format includes Bible study as part of every gathering. The thirty-minute format allows participants to use the Bible study as part of their ongoing journal work outside of the group's time together. Both formats include time for relaxation, prayer, a continuing story about the woman in search of her heart, quiet journaling, and opportunities for sharing. Your particular group may decide which format best suits your needs and schedules.

Questions and Answers

Now, turn to a woman sitting beside you—a different person than last time—introduce yourself, and ask, "What questions do you have about *Heart to Heart*?" We will pause for three minutes for the two of you to converse freely. Then, those who wish will have the opportunity to share their questions with the entire group. I will let you know when thirty seconds remain.

> Keep time for three minutes, announcing when thirty seconds remain. When time is up, call the group back together.

Time is up. What questions do you have about *Heart to Heart*?

> As the women ask questions, write the questions on newsprint, numbering each one. Try to write each question exactly as stated. Do not repeat the question. Repeating keeps the women focused on you instead of on one another.

For some answers, we will be turning to the *Guidebook.*

> Again, hold up a copy of the *Guidebook.* Be familiar with its contents. Address the questions asked in the order that is easiest for you. Circle each number on the newsprint as you begin to address that question.

Registration Cards

> If you are using the multiple groups format, which allows women to attend any scheduled *Heart to Heart* gathering that fits her schedule for a given week or month, pass out registration cards (made from page 192) and pencils. If you are not using this model, skip to the next section, "Be-Attitudes."

I am passing out registration cards. Because there will be multiple *Heart to Heart* groups, you have the option of attending one of several gatherings scheduled each week or month. Simply plug into the gathering that best suits your schedule. For example, if you have a dental appointment on Tuesday morning, when one group is gathering, you may attend any other gathering during the week—morning, afternoon, or evening; in a home, at the church, or wherever the group may be gathering.

Since groups will be gathering at various times and various sites, we need to know what days and times are most convenient for you. Please note your preferences on the registration card.

> Pause while the women fill out the cards. Collect all the cards, even from those who say they cannot complete the card at this time. Tell them that they may call you later, and that you will complete the information on the card for them. When you have collected all the cards, continue.

A schedule will be printed soon. You will receive a postcard listing the days, times, and gathering places for all *Heart to Heart* groups. Or you may get the schedule by calling (person's name or office) at (telephone number). The schedule also will be printed weekly in the church bulletin and/or newsletter as well as posted on the bulletin board and, when possible, outside the doors of the gathering rooms.

Be-Attitudes

In preparation for the second half of this introductory session, here are a few "Be-Attitudes" to consider.

> Pass out copies of "Be-Attitudes," page 187.

I invite you to read them aloud with me.

> Read slowly with the group.

Introducing Sacred Story Bible Study and From the Heart Journal: A Personal PrayerJournal for Women

> The following Bible study begins the second half of the introductory session.

We will now participate in an important component of *Heart to Heart* called Sacred Story Bible Study. This twenty- to thirty-minute Bible study is a part of every one-hour gathering; groups meeting for thirty minutes do the Bible study as part of their ongoing journaling at home. Today we will be sampling the Opening Hearts Sacred Story Bible Study method, one of four interactive methods used in *Heart to Heart* to explore stories of Jesus' encounters with women as well as stories about women told by Jesus. The Sacred Story Bible Study approach helps us hear God's Word and apply it to our hearts and lives. It opens us so that we may gain insights and hear God's voice through the reflections of others. Sacred Story Bible Study is not a discussion group. The ancient stories will meet us in our own story as we reflect by reading, writing, and listening. We will be using a sample journal page reproduced on colored paper.

> (Note: If you would like to provide more information about the four different methods, see pages 42–43.)

Break into small groups of three to five persons. Choose women whom you know the least. Circle your chairs and sit knee to knee.

Spread out around the room.

> While this is being accomplished, pass out copies of "Opening Hearts Sacred Story Bible Study: Great Is Your Faith! (Introductory Session)," pages 188–90 (duplicated on front and back of a sheet of colored paper).

Introduce yourselves to one another and decide who will be the facilitator. The facilitator simply keeps time and reads through each step as it appears on the handout. She does nothing else except participate along with the rest of the group.

> Pause until this is accomplished.

I will be available to answer any questions. This Bible study takes twenty to thirty minutes. When your group finishes, you are invited to continue with quiet conversation. I will be coming around to answer additional questions you may have and to check your progress. You will be dismissed from your small group.

> Check on the progress of each group. Intervene only if a group gets bogged down or a conversation erupts before they have completed the Bible study. You also may remind participants to use "I" statements as they respond. Be available as the women prepare to leave. Thank them for coming. There is no formal group ending.

Follow-up

After the introductory session, review the registration cards. Determine the best days, times, and places to hold groups. If possible, solicit a group coordinator for each *Heart to Heart* group. Work with the group coordinators to make arrangements for childcare and facility use. Print a schedule of all *Heart to Heart* gatherings and send copies, along with details regarding childcare and any other pertinent information, to all who attended the introductory session. Also post the schedule in publications, on bulletin boards, and outside gathering rooms if possible. Work with group coordinators as necessary to purchase or order the appropriate number of resources, and begin securing equipment and supplies needed for the gatherings. (When ordering resources, remember to allow at least two weeks for delivery. Schedule the first gatherings accordingly.)

Sacred Story Bible Study: An Introduction

Overview

*S*acred Story Bible Study is a major component of *Heart to Heart*. This twenty- to thirty-minute study is a part of every sixty-minute gathering. Groups that meet for thirty minutes may use the Bible study as part of their ongoing journal work outside of the group's time together. Another option for thirty-minute groups is to use Sacred Story Bible Study at every other gathering, alternating between the material in the *Guidebook* and the Bible study. This extends the number of sessions to twenty-four.

Sacred Story Bible Study is a unique way for women new to biblical stories to experience the power of the gospel in an interactive way. And long-time students of the Bible will hear God's Word with a new ear. The study of Jesus and the women in his life and his parables creates an intimacy that is authentic; it also respects the authority of each person's voice as she considers how God influences her life. This Bible study process grows more powerful with each use. The Word breaks hearts open. The gospel has power!

Four Methods

The four methods of Bible study used in *Heart to Heart* are centered in "matters that are divine." These spiritually-centered methods provide an excellent tool to help women find spiritual nourishment in the midst of their busy lives. All of the Bible studies offer step-by-step directions, making them easy to use. Using all four methods during your twelve-week *Heart to Heart* experience will lend variety to your group's gatherings. Not only may you use them in your gatherings, you also may adapt them for your own personal devotions.

Although the steps of each method vary somewhat, they follow a similar pattern, which includes reading, reflecting, and talking. The final step of each method is prayer. The four methods are as follows:

1. Opening Hearts includes reading the Scripture together and then journaling individually with a specifically stated focus.

2. Imagine This! invites you to close your eyes and place yourself in the biblical scene as the Scripture is read.

3. Praying the Scripture is taken from the writings of Madame Guyon, a Christian woman of the seventeenth century. Using this method, you read the Scripture together, journal your reflections, and share your thoughts with one another.

4. Responsive Listening is an oral tradition Bible study that leads you in reading the Scripture together three times. After each reading, you pause to discern aloud God's will for your lives. (Note: This Bible study method also is used in the group resource *SpiritGifts: One Spirit, Many Gifts,* by Patricia D. Brown. Abingdon Press, 1996.)

Monastic practices call these methods *collatio,* the "bringing together" of a shared supper. They are a gathering of friends and stories around a table, bringing together connections related to a Scripture text. The methods have been used widely by the world church; in retreats; by workers at lunch breaks; and in base communities of developing countries, where Bible study, prayer, singing, personal compassion, and social action often merge into one.

Listening, not talking, is the key. *Lectio divina,* which means "divine reading," emphasizes hearing the message of the text, listening to others' reflections, and taking to heart what God is saying to individuals as well as to the group as a whole. Again, this approach is different from a discussion group; it emphasizes listening and reflecting on the sacred text.

Time

Each of the four methods of Bible study is designed to take approximately twenty to thirty minutes.

Group Size

When there are more than five persons in the full gathering, divide into smaller groups of three to five for the Bible study. Groups larger than five may overwhelm one another with too much input. Larger groups also increase the time required for the Bible study, causing the study to extend beyond thirty minutes.

Room SetUp

Form groups of three to five. Arrange the chairs in a circle, so that the participants in each group are sitting knee to knee. Do not sit around tables or use tables to lean on or circle around. Space the groups around the room so that the women in each group may hear one another clearly.

Facilitating the Study

Ask for a volunteer to convene each small group. It is best if the leading role is passed to someone other than the person who facilitated the previous Bible study. One woman in each group serves as the facilitator for the entire Bible study session.

The facilitator begins by reading the directions aloud to the entire group, unless the directions indicate otherwise. Reading through the entire study process before beginning is especially helpful the first time. This gives everyone an overview.

After the overview, the facilitator reads the steps again one by one, stopping after each so that the group may follow the instructions. She reads each step as written, without adding comments. While they do as instructed, she keeps time and indicates when they should move on to the next step, making sure the group stays within the time parameters. No one is "called on" to share. Instead, the group waits for volunteers. Women in the group may choose to pass. This decision should be respected. In time, everyone will become more comfortable with silences.

Group Processing

You will discover a great deal about yourselves and about group process from the dynamics of Sacred Story Bible Study. For starters, here are a few "helpful hints."

"I" statements are important. They force the speaker to care for the splinter in her own eye and leave the mote in the other person's eye to God. This is not a narcissistic, belly-button-gazing "I" statement, but an important "I" statement that leads us to accountability for the choices we make in our own lives. Habit often leads us to use general statements when talking ("Everyone thinks that . . ." or "We all know . . ."). The facilitator may remind everyone to use "I" statements until the group grows accustomed to doing so.

When first using Sacred Story Bible Study, some of you may find that you are preoccupied by what you want to say. *Over time, you will learn to turn off your preoccupation with your own agenda and center in on what others say.* Others of you may feel the need to explain your statements, fearful that you may be misinterpreted. As you learn to hear one another nonjudgmentally, trust will develop and this defensiveness will lessen. We women often look for signs of approval as we speak; Sacred Story Bible Study frees us from the need to seek approval. It also creates a safe space for both the introvert and the extrovert to share. The first is not left out, and the second does not dominate.

Still others of you may have the urge to "jump in" and comment on what others say. If this is you, you have difficulty just listening. You will benefit by sitting quietly and observing your reactions. You may ask yourself: Isn't my reaction to what my *Heart to Heart* friend is saying interesting?

Sacred Story Bible Study creates an intimacy that is authentic, not superficial. And it allows for comfortable, healing silence. Don't rush to fill such silences with sound.

Part 2

Getting
Into
Heart to Heart

Gathering 1

Heartbeat

Note: Music sets the mood and helps women make the transition into the circle. Use selections from any of the three categories included in the "Bibliography of Suggested Music"—"Meditative," "Music for Movement," and "Sing-along"—depending on how you're feeling at the moment. See the Appendix, pages 200–03. You also may use other appropriate songs.

Circle of Hearts

Note: One woman begins the gathering by reading aloud to the group. Read at an unhurried pace.

Welcome to *Heart to Heart*, Gathering 1. It is good to be taking this special time from our hectic schedules to be here. Together we will learn how to have heart, enjoy lighthearted laughter, and experience heartfelt care. We will see that our hearts, centered in God's love, are what *Heart to Heart* is all about.

Because there is no prep time involved in *Heart to Heart*, each woman here is a guest. *Heart to Heart* understands our busy schedules; the gatherings are designed so that they may be completed in thirty minutes. There also is the option of extending to a sixty-minute gathering so that Bible study may be included, if that is desirable to the group.

Everything that follows is to be read aloud, with the exception of "notes" to the reader that are underlined. We will do whatever the instructions tell us to do at the time they instruct us to do it. If the instructions say to stop and do an activity, indicated by the symbol 🛑, we will do it. We will wait until everyone has completed the activity before proceeding. All we have to do is keep listening and following the simple step-by-step instructions in this *Guidebook*.

Like women who gather in the kitchen or the workplace to accomplish a common goal, each one pitching in to get the job done, we will share leadership. Whenever we see this heart symbol, ♥, the role of facilitator passes to the next person. For example, I will stop reading at the end of this sentence and pass the leadership task to the person on my right. ♥

Anytime any of us does not wish to participate, we simply say, "Pass," and the role of facilitator moves to the next woman. Let's stop right now and, all together, say, **"Pass."** 🛑 See, that was easy. During times of sharing, we will be passing a hand-sized heart around the circle to designate a person's turn to speak. Again, if you do not wish to share, simply continue passing the heart around the circle. Because this style may be different from other groups we have experienced, it may be awkward at first. But if we keep an open mind, our hearts will be blessed.

If we have not already done so, let us gather around a central table. We will not sit *at* the table but will circle our chairs *around* the table. The table is our focus center. 🛑 Now I will take the articles for our gathering from the supply box and arrange them on the focus center: a cloth covering; a candle and matches (or a lighter); a heart-shaped box containing small wooden hearts; a hand-sized heart; a bell; nametags and tag holders; and wide-edged felt-tip pens (one for every two women). 🛑 ♥

Take a nametag and holder from the table. 🛑 To symbolize that this

50

is a shared adventure, do not write your own name on your nametag. Instead, turn to another group member, tell her your name, and ask her to write your name on the tag in **BIG BOLD LETTERS** and slip it into the tag holder. Have her pin your nametag high on your shoulder so that it is easy to see. Then do the same for her. As you do this, share words of welcome with each other. When everyone has completed the task, we will continue the gathering. 🛑 ♥

Heartbeat

Note: To prepare yourselves for "Heartwarmers," a time of prayer and relaxation, choose from the selections in the "Meditative" category in the "Bibliography of Suggested Music," pages 200–03, or play another song of your choice.

Heartwarmers

I am moving now to light the candle on our focus center. 🛑
As I light the candle, join me in saying these words from our teacher, Jesus. Repeat each line aloud after me: 🛑

> **Come to me, all you that are weary** 🛑
> **and are carrying heavy burdens,** 🛑
> **and I will give you rest.** 🛑
> **Take my yoke upon you,** 🛑
> **and learn from me;** 🛑
> **for I am gentle** 🛑
> **and humble in heart,** 🛑
> **and you will find rest for your souls.** 🛑
>
> _(Matthew 11:28-29)_

Let us pause for prayer. Pray with me. 🛑

Loving God, make our hearts a dwelling place for your love. May your Spirit fill us with care so that we may share warmth with the world. Amen.

Note: The facilitator may not be able to participate fully in the following relaxation exercise. Pause for at least ten seconds at each 🛑.

Right now, all you have to do is relax and breathe. Begin by placing your feet flat on the floor. 🛑 Free your hands and laps of any articles. 🛑 As silly as it sounds, most of the time we breathe shallow breaths, forgetting how to breathe deeply. Take a deep breath in through your nose, fill up your lungs, and blow the air out through your nose. 🛑 Now do it again, this time breathing like a baby. First, push your stomach out as you take a deep breath in through your nose. 🛑 Then blow the air out through your nose as you contract your stomach. 🛑 Close your eyes and take three more slow, deep breaths, remembering each time to expand your stomach as you breath in and contract your stomach as you breath out. 🛑 When you are finished, open your eyes and we will continue. 🛑 ♥

A Heart-Centered Story

We begin our heart-centered journey with a story. This story is about a woman on a spiritual quest. Like a soap opera, it is a continuing story. Today we will read Chapter 1. We will go around the circle and take turns reading the story aloud. Remember, you have the option to say, "Pass," if you prefer not to read aloud. Please read slowly and thoughtfully.

The Quest of the Woman in Search of Her Heart

Chapter 1

As our story begins, we meet a woman who has lost her heart. One morning she awoke and found it gone. The space inside, where it once beat, is now empty. She has a hole where her heart used to be.

She vaguely remembers it being there the last time she checked. When had that been? Was it there yesterday, when she packed her daughter off to college? Perhaps it was a week ago during the fiasco of the fund-raising supper, when colleagues who had promised to help failed to show. Surely it couldn't have been a whole month since she'd checked. That would mean it had been before she broke a luncheon date with a long-time friend because her schedule overflowed. Certainly not a full year! That would mean she hadn't seen her heart since her mother's funeral. Bewildered, she wonders how she could have gone this long without realizing her heart was missing. But, thinking back, she can't recall when she last saw it. ♥

She scours each room in search of her heart. *I've just mislaid it,* she thinks, *under a stack of magazines. Or maybe I filed it away with last quarter's financial records.* A diligent search from attic to basement provides no clues. *I hope it wasn't accidentally left behind when I transferred to this division,* she thinks. *Perhaps I've left pieces of my heart here and there and everywhere. That might be good. It might be easier to trace my way back, if I need to.* She falls into bed exhausted, turns out the light, and waits for sleep. ♥

Restless, she tosses from side to side. She punches her rock-like pillow but fails to make it comfortable. Her eyes remain wide open as her mind races first to one thing and then another. Are the doors locked? Is the cat in? It is now 11 o'clock. Does she know where her children are? ♥

Then she remembers all the other things she has lost through the years: a favorite necklace, her virginity, matching socks, the cheerleading try-outs, her friend to death, a husband through divorce, her house in the settlement, her size-eight waistline, a couple of jobs, both parents. The list runs on. Seeking comfort, she pulls the blanket over her head, hiding in its tent. *A person without a heart can become very cold, she thinks as she drifts off to sleep.* ♥

Bang! The woman bolts upright, sharply awake. Perhaps she has been disturbed by a dream, although no fragments of it linger. Another day without a heart. She looks expectantly around the house, but her heart has not returned. *I'll make a list of persons who might have it and places where it might be,* she thinks. And she does. First, she checks with her best friend. She missed their after-work date a while back and meant to call but never got around to it. Has her friend seen her heart? No, she hasn't, the friend replies, but she promises to check her sofa in case it has fallen between the cushions. "You know how easily things slip through the cracks," she says. ♥

The woman calls her sister and has to reassure her twice that it really is her calling—so infrequent are the contacts between them. That was a wasted call. Her boss suggests she check her jacket, for she is known for wearing her heart on her sleeve. A quick call to the church. No help there—just a suggestion that she pray about it. Pray about it? Get real. How can she leave such a thing to chance?

She decides to intensify her search. Grabbing her car keys and purse, she sets out to find her heart. *To be continued. . . .* ♥

From the Heart Journal: A Personal Prayer Journal for Women

Now I will pass out copies of the personal prayer journal we will be using throughout *Heart to Heart*. It is called *From the Heart Journal: A Personal Prayer Journal for Women.* 🛑 In our journals, we will write our heartfelt reflections and thoughts. There are pages for us to use in our gatherings and pages for us to use at home. Now that we have read chapter 1 of "The Quest of the Woman in Search of Her Heart," we will take time to write in our journals.

Whenever we write as a group activity, we will use periods of silence. In *Heart to Heart*, we call this exercise "fasting from speech." You will need to find some space for yourself. You may want to move to another part of the room, another room, or even outside to write. This fasting from speech helps us learn to listen to our hearts and to allow God to speak to our hearts. ♥

Fasting from speech helps each of us to see what comes between us and God. There may be some things from which we need to abstain in order to make time for God. Let's stop for a minute and name out loud some of the things that take up our time, things from which we might "fast" in order to make room for God. _Note: Allow approximately one minute for random sharing; then continue._ 🛑

Some days we may decide to abstain from newspapers and television, which overwhelm us. We may choose to turn off the computer and let voice mail or answering machines take phone messages. When the kids are driving us crazy, we may pause from our families. At any time we may choose to fast from speech, step away from it all, take a long walk, gain a keener perspective, or take some time apart so that we may love again—so that we may find compassion for others. Jesus often went to a quiet place away from his friends. We also need times away from it all. We need times of silent reflection. ♥

Our reflections may provide clues as to where we may begin looking for our hearts. Remember, our journals are private. We will share from them only as we choose.

Turn in your journal to "Cracks in My Life," page 20. 🛑 We will fast from speech for ten minutes as we write. I will let you know when time is up by sounding a bell. We then will break our time of silence with a unison prayer. Remember not to speak until the prayer. _Note: Ring the bell after ten minutes._ 🛑

You've Got to Have Heart

Now that we've come together again, join me in saying aloud the following prayer: 🛑

> **Silence is golden, and so rare in our lives.**
> **What a gift to have ten minutes all to ourselves.**
> **Thank you, God, for making us wise women, ready to receive.**
> **Amen.**

We are now invited to share as we are comfortable. I am moving to take the hand-sized heart from the focus center. 🛑 We will pass the heart around the circle as we share. When the heart comes to you, it is your turn to share. When you are finished, pass the heart to the woman on your right. We will continue in this manner until everyone has had the opportunity to share. If anyone does not wish to share, she simply passes the heart. When we are finished, we will return the heart to the focus center. Since I am holding the heart, I will share first. _Note: If this is a thirty-minute gathering, you will not have time to discuss or share your_ *journal entries. Instead, move on to the next section. If the gathering is planned for sixty or more minutes, stop and share as previously instructed. When the heart makes its way back to you, return it to the focus center.* 🛑 ♥

Sacred Story Bible Study

Note: If this is a thirty-minute gathering, or if your group will not be doing the Bible study together for another reason, move on to the next section. Take some time this week to read and reflect on the Sacred Story.

In this exercise, we will use the "Opening Hearts" method of "Sacred Story Bible Study". First we will read the text. Next we will write in our journals. Then we will listen to one another's reflections. In this way, we will search our hearts and discern what God is saying to us. This is not a time for discussion. Instead, the study emphasizes listening and reflecting on the Scriptures.

If there are more than five women in our full group, we will divide into small circles of three to five by choosing women whom we know the least. We will space our groups around the room and circle our chairs so that we are sitting knee to knee. Each group will need to choose a facilitator, who will guide her group through the entire Sacred Story exercise. We will remain in quiet reflection and prayer until all of the groups are finished. 🛑 ♥

Opening Hearts
Note: The small group facilitator begins reading here.

Turn in your journal to page 22, "Opening Hearts Sacred Story Bible Study: New Birth." First I will read all the way through the step-by-step directions aloud. 🛑

Now I will read the directions a second time, pausing at each step as indicated and appropriate so that we may work through the process together.

Note: Follow the directions on pages 22–25 in your journal to complete the study. When finished, return quietly to the larger circle and fast from speech until everyone has completed the study. 🛑 ♥

You've Got to Have Heart

I am moving to take the heart box from our focus center. (STOP)

We will pass the heart box around the circle. Each person will close her eyes as she takes one "message from the heart" from the box. We will wait until everyone has a message(STOP). Now we will go around the circle and say aloud the word printed on the heart. I will start. (STOP)

Now, consider the word printed on the heart you hold. Write it in your journal on page 26, "Message from the Heart."(STOP) As you think about the word, write your initial reaction to the word in the space provided in your journal. We will pause for one minute to fast from speech. I will let you know when time is up. _Note: Signal to the group that time is up after one minute._ (STOP)

I am moving to take the hand-sized heart from the focus center. (STOP) As we did earlier in the gathering, we will pass the heart around the circle as we share. When the heart comes to you, it is your turn to share your thoughts with the group. Remember, share at your comfort level. Trust your inner voice. Be brief, keeping your answer to one minute or less. If you do not wish to share, simply pass the heart. When we are finished, we will return the heart to the focus center. Since I am holding the heart, I will share first. _Note: After you have shared, pass the heart to the woman on your right. When all others in the circle have shared as they choose and the heart has made its way back to you, return it to the focus center and continue with the following._ (STOP)

Take your heart-word home with you. Until we meet again, consider the questions found in your journal on pages 26 and 27, and record your reflections. ♥

A Hearty Goodbye

We prepare to leave by reading aloud together the following prayer, which helps us take an earnest look at ourselves. **STOP**

Lord, you know I bring a great deal of knowledge to this group. Keep me from thinking that I must declare myself on every subject. Give me the wisdom to know when to speak and when to keep silent, when to share and when to listen. Teach me the wondrous lesson that, from time to time, I could be wrong.

Let me not mistake superficial confidences for genuine intimacy. And help me remember that sometimes confession doesn't fill the chasm but only widens it.

Make me deeply caring, but not meddlesome; charitable, but not bossy; loving, but not mothering. It seems a pity not to use all the wisdom and experience I've gained through the years. But, you know, I want a few friends in the end.

So help me to stop and pray, to talk less and listen more. And more than all this, let me keep growing and living in ways that bring everyone closer to heaven. Amen. ♥

Gathering 2 will take place on *(date/s)* at *(time/s and place/s)*. _Note: If you are using the multiple groups format, explain that participants may attend any scheduled gathering. If the group needs to discuss meeting dates, times, and places, do so now._ **STOP**

Take your message from the heart home with you, and bring it back to the next gathering. You will use it again. Don't panic if you lose your heart in the interval. We all do at times, you know. If you can't find your heart, just come as you are. ♥

Note: The facilitator of the following relaxation exercise may not be able to participate fully. Pause at least ten seconds or longer at each **STOP** .

Before we leave, set aside all your materials so that your hands are free. **STOP** Close your eyes. **STOP** Place your feet flat on the floor. **STOP** Take a long, deep breath and hold it for a count of ten. **STOP** Now blow it out. **STOP** When everyone has opened her eyes, we will stand. **STOP**

I cradle the heart box in my hands. **STOP** Like the material it is made of, we are reminded that we, too, are both fragile and strong. As we pass it from person to person, we show the bond that will grow among us as we share our light, wisdom, and strength with one another. Turn to the person standing to your right and, as you hand her the heart box, say:

Go, knowing you are loved.

Remember to take off your nametag and place it on the focus center as you leave. As I extinguish the candle, go in God's love. **STOP**

Gathering 2

Heartbeat

Circle of Hearts

Note: One woman begins the gathering by reading the following aloud to the group. Remember to read slowly, leaving space for silence. For more detailed reminders on how to open and conduct a Heart to Heart *gathering, refer to "Getting Started," pages 28–32.*

Welcome to this second gathering of *Heart to Heart*. As we did in our first gathering, we will share the role of facilitator. We will take turns reading aloud the step-by-step instructions. Remember, we are to read everything aloud except notes to the reader appearing in italics. When it is your turn to read, slow your reading so that there is time for silent reflection. Anytime you do not wish to participate, simply say "Pass," and the role of facilitator will move to the next woman.

No one person is the teacher or leader here. Instead, we will work together as a whole. This allows everyone to share ownership of the process. Leadership is not a role placed on a single individual but a series of tasks shared by everyone. Whenever we see the heart symbol, ♥, the role of facilitator passes to the next person. Whoever is reading stops, and the person on her right continues. Whenever we see this symbol, **STOP**, we are to stop and complete the instructions. ♥

If we have not already done so, let us circle our chairs around a central table—our focus center. **STOP** Now I will take the articles for our gathering from the supply box and arrange them on the focus center: a cloth covering, a candle and matches (or a lighter), a heart-shaped box, a hand-sized heart, nametags and tag holders, a wide-edged felt-tip pen, a bell, and a long taper candle. **STOP** ♥

Each person may now select another person's nametag from the table. Do not take your own. Then walk over to the person to whom the tag belongs, pin the nametag on her, and greet her warmly. When everyone has finished and returned to her seat, we will continue. **STOP**

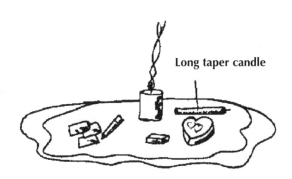

Long taper candle

Heartbeat

Note: To set the mood for the following prayer ritual, choose a song from the "Meditative" category of the "Bibliography of Suggested Music," page 200–03 in the Appendix, or choose other appropriate music. Play the selection as background music during "Heartwarmers."

Heartwarmers

On Sunday mornings, our churches light candles, signifying the start of worship. The candle I am moving to light marks the beginning of our time together and reminds us of our purpose as a community. I light the candle as a symbolic act that signifies we claim this special time and place. **STOP** This lighted candle symbolizes our decision to set this time apart. We celebrate this moment and one another. This gathering is a celebration! ♥

Let's take a moment to relax, so that we may enter more fully into the celebration. We will slow down and breathe in ways that will help us let go of tension. This deep breathing exercise is one we may use in our everyday lives. The next time we prepare to make a dreaded phone call or begin a conversation we've been putting off or blow our cool, let us stop and remember how to breathe. When we are anxious, we breathe shallow breaths. We forget how to breathe deeply. ♥

Note: The person facilitating the following relaxation exercise may not be able to participate fully. Pause at least ten seconds or longer at each **STOP**.

Place your feet flat on the floor. **STOP** Free your hands and lap of all objects.**STOP** Close your eyes as I read the following instructions.**STOP** Take a deep breath in through your nose. Fill up your lungs. **STOP** Now, slowly blow the air out through your nose.**STOP**

Do you remember watching an infant breathe as she sleeps? This time, breathe in like an infant. Extend your stomach muscles out as you take a deep breath in through your nose. **STOP** Now, blow the air out through your nose.**STOP** Remain with your eyes closed and take three more slow, deep breaths, remembering each time to expand your stomach as you breathe in and contract your stomach as you breathe out. When you finish, open your eyes and we will continue. **STOP** ♥

It is good to take time from our hectic lives to be together. It is not wasting time. Spiritual work is as important as any task or project we undertake. Spending time with God and with other women on the spiritual journey is important work. For the following minutes, we will slow down and will not feel guilty about "wasting time." ♥

When we follow God's command to love our neighbors as ourselves, we take time to know ourselves—these persons we are to love. This love of self is not narcissistic, selfish, or full of "me-ism." Instead, it is a genuine concern for ourselves that enables us to extend our love to God and others. In this love, each of us can be a person who is healthy, whole, and Christ-centered—a person with plenty to give to others. ♥

Heartbeat

Note: Choose a song from those listed in the "Sing-along" category on pages 202–03 of the "Bibliography of Suggested Music," or choose another appropriate song. Play the song and sing along on the refrain.

You've Got to Have Heart

Turn in your journal to pages 26 and 27, "Message from the Heart." At the first gathering, you received a small heart from the heart-shaped box. Written on the heart was a word, a message from the heart. You were invited to live with that word until this gathering. You also were asked to do some journaling. In a few minutes you will be invited to share with the group. Let's pause for five minutes of silent reflection so that you may review or complete your responses on pages 26 and 27 in your journal. I will let you know when time is up. _Note: Ring the bell when five minutes have expired._ 🛑

I am moving to take the hand-sized heart from the focus center. 🛑 As we did at our first gathering, we will pass the heart around the circle as we share. When the heart comes to you, it is your turn to share. As you speak, remind yourself to use "I" and "me" statements, not "we" and "they" statements. Remember to share only at your comfort level and to be concise and to the point. Trust your inner voice. If you do not wish to share, simply pass the heart. When we are finished, we will return the heart to the focus center. Since I am holding the heart, I will share first. _Note: After sharing your own writings, pass the heart to the woman on your right. When all others in the circle have shared as they choose and the heart has made its way back to you, return it to the focus center._ 🛑 ♥

A Heart-Centered Story

The Quest of the Woman in Search of Her Heart

Chapter 2

In Chapter 1 of our story, we were introduced a woman who had lost her heart. Let us journey with her now as she follows the advice of a friend and travels far into the country seeking help. As you continue the story, remember to read slowly and thoughtfully.

––––––––––––––

The woman who lost her heart has a first name: Questa. Questa is French and means "forever seeking," a good description of her life. At one time she remembered having a last name, too. Her name has changed so many times through the years that she finally has abandoned the thought of hanging her identity on it. Questa suits her fine. ♥

Questa has been driving for four hours, and it is getting dark. She is tired. Why is she making this trip? She still isn't sure. All she knows is that her girlfriend Sally gave her this address. Sally told her: "You will meet a wise woman. Her name is Sage. She will give you further directions."

Finally, as she is driving on a country road, she spots a mailbox. It has a heart painted on its side, just as her friend told her it would. She walks up the path and onto the porch. She knocks on the door. She waits. Is anyone here? The occupant must know she has better things to do than stand in drafty entranceways. The door opens. This must be Sage. ♥

Questa first notices Sage's eyes: deep pools of brown full of something she cannot name. They make her seem older than she is. Is this Sage, as her name suggests, one who is wise through experience and reflection? Sage invites her to step inside, and Questa scans the room. Mostly she notices the earthen pottery and the smell of freshly baked bread. But something is not quite right. What? ♥

"You are an artist," Questa says.

Sage nods. The pottery is her work. Every piece is special.

"I tried my hand at pottery once myself," says Questa. For Questa, pottery making had become a chore. She had signed up for a class and had paid close attention to the instructor, but she hadn't been able to get the clay centered on the wheel. After a couple of weeks, she had stopped attending.

Sage seems to be waiting. *Should I say something more—blurt out my troubles to this stranger?* Questa wonders. She stalls. "My friend seems to think you can help me," she says finally.

"Sally and I are long-time friends," Sage says. "I knew her when we were both struggling—just beginning our work. We learned a lot from each other." ♥

Sage is waiting again. Now what? Questa has always been good at chitchat, but now it doesn't seem appropriate. What is she supposed to say?

"Do you feel comfortable here?" Sage asks.

"No," replies Questa. Another awkward pause. "Perhaps I shouldn't have come. I didn't mean to waste your time."

"Have some coffee," says Sage. Questa watches Sage pour coffee into earthenware cups. "You've had a very busy life?" Sage comments. It is more of a question than a statement.

"All my days," Questa responds. The coffee tastes good. ♥

"Why?" Sage asks.

"What do you mean, 'Why?' " Questa quizzes back.

"Why have you been so busy?" asks Sage again.

Questa has never thought much about it. She hesitates, then answers slowly, "Why is anyone busy? It's what people do. It's life. It's who I am."

"Do you like who you are?" asks Sage.

"I'm fine." Defensive, Questa lies. Sage has to know it is a lie. Does she? Maybe not. "At least I used to think I was," Questa adds. "Sometimes I think I'm OK." ♥

"What's different?" asks Sage.

Questa hesitates. Should she really tell this stranger the truth? Why not? She has nothing to lose. What is this person to her? She begins. "A year ago I knew what I wanted. My life was on track. I had it all figured out, and I knew how to get there. People saw me as creative and talented. Up-and-comers sought my advice. I was in the know. Politically astute. With it."

"And now?" Sage draws her out.

"I'm not sure," Questa says. "All I know now is that it's not working anymore."

"You're feeling tired? Betrayed?" says Sage, sounding as if she cares. Perhaps she understands. Then why does she make Questa feel so on edge?

Questa presses on. "It's as if I'm at the railroad station and this speeding train comes roaring by. I keep trying to jump on one of the passing cars, but the train never slows. I'm running alongside with all my might, but I can't seem to catch up enough to get on. I run faster and faster, and just when I think I will make it, the train pulls ahead even faster." ♥

"You need to stop running," Sage says simply.

"I didn't need to drive four hours to learn that," retorts Questa. Sage must hear her impatience. "I've tried everything," Questa continues. "Time-management workshops, videotapes, stress management seminars, yoga, counseling. I keep my priority list on my refrigerator and subscribe to self-help magazines," Questa concludes. ♥

Why is Sage so silent? Does Sage think the steps she has taken are stupid? That her failure is her fault?

Questa plunges on. "I use the latest make-life-easier technology—microwave food, on-line e-mail, in-home shopping. I keep myself abreast of the world with *Newsweek*, the local newspaper, and *Jeopardy.*"

Sage smiles. "Why do you do all these things?"

Her smile grates on Questa's nerves. She feels her insides contract. Is Sage laughing at her?

Sage's face turns serious. "What do you want?"

The question stings. *What does she want?* Questa's mouth grows dry. "My family, work, and community are my life. They are what I've always wanted. But it's not fun anymore. I dread getting up in the morning. My 'to do' list grows longer and longer. For the first time in my life, I feel like a failure." ♥

"What's not working?" Sage asks.

Questa tells about her need to feel valued. She tells how the more she does, the more her work is taken for granted. She says she needs support, yet unrelenting demands continue to pile on to her already strained schedule. Things seem to be coming apart. She has never felt this way before.

Sage says that she's been there, that she understands.

Where has Sage been? Does she really understand? Questa wonders. She wants to respond and opens her mouth to do so. No words come. ♥

"And your heart?" Sage asks.

So Sage has known all along about her missing heart. Questa feels ashamed. She wants to escape, to get away from this crazy woman. But she can't move.

"My heart?" Questa stammers.

"Yes, your heart." Sage's tone is strong, searching. It is as if she is asking an everyday question.

"What do you mean?" asks Questa.

"Your heart. That wholeness within that brings together all that is important and of value to you. That deep inner part that longs to be at one with God, one with yourself, and one with others," says Sage.

The woman without a heart is dying inside. It was a mistake for her to come here. ♥

"It is as if you are sleepwalking," Sage continues. "Each day is what you make it," she says in a quiet voice. "If you believe you have no choices, you won't. Life simply carries you—perhaps where you would choose not to go. If you don't wake up, if you live life numb, others will make choices for you. But know the choices will not be in your best interests. They will be in theirs. You are going through the motions, but your heart isn't there." ♥

She has driven four hours for this? Questa feels the hurt build. This whole conversation has taken a wrong turn somewhere. Ridiculously, tears fill her eyes as she tells Sage what she feels. "Look, I don't have time for this. I need a fix, not a riddle. I don't need your prying. The truth is, I have a hole where my heart used to be. Maybe I lost it. Maybe someone stole it. And now it hurts all the time, and I don't know if it can be fixed. Sometimes I even forget it's gone." ♥

Their eyes meet. "How do you hope to make your life different? More sweat? More control? More self-help tricks? A new mantra?" Sage asks.

"Maybe some compassion," Questa shoots back. From where did that come? It just slipped out. ♥

Sage says, "Compassion comes. First, you have to ask your heart."

Questa can feel the blood rush to her face. Why doesn't she just walk out? "How can I ask my heart if I can't even find it?"

"Can't you?" Sage asks.

"That's what I've come to you for. My friend says you can help me find it," says Questa, in tears.

"Do you want to find it?" inquires Sage.

What a stupid question. "Of course I do," says Questa. ♥

Then, in a low, quiet voice, Sage says to Questa, "I can't tell you how to find your heart. Only you know where it is. No one can make the journey to claim it for you. Would you want someone to choose your path? Decide your end? No one can find your heart. Not your therapist, not your boss, not your pastor. Only you know the way back to your heart." *To be continued. . . .* ♥

From the Heart Journal:
A Personal Prayer Journal for Women

Now turn in your journal to page 28, "My 'Stuff'." 🛑 For the next ten minutes we will fast from speech as we listen to our hearts and to God's word to us. During this period of silence, we will follow the instructions in our prayer journals and take time apart to reflect and write. Remember, our journals are private. We will share only what we choose. *Note: Ring the bell when ten minutes have expired.*🛑

You've Got to Have Heart

Time is up. I am moving to take the hand-sized heart from the focus center. 🛑 We will pass the heart around the circle as we share. When the heart comes to you, it is your turn to share one item from your list with the group. When you are finished, pass the heart to the woman on your right. We will continue in this manner until everyone has had the opportunity to share. When we are finished, we will return the heart to the focus center. Since I am holding the heart, I will share first. *Note: After you share, pass the heart to the woman on your right. When all others in the circle who wish to share have done so and the heart has made its way back to you, return the heart to the focus center.* ♥ 🛑

Sacred Story Bible Study

Note: If this is a thirty-minute gathering, or if your group will not be doing the Bible study together for another reason, move on to the next section. Take some time this week to read and reflect on the Sacred Story.

Our goal in reading the Sacred Stories is to grow into a deeper, more authentic relationship with God—not simply to learn the content of a biblical text. In this gathering we will use the Imagine This! method of Sacred Story Bible Study, which centers on transformation rather than information. As we will discover, it is best suited for use with narrative stories.

If there are more than five women in our full group, we will divide into small circles of three to five by choosing women whom we know the least. We will space our groups around the room and circle our chairs so that we are sitting knee to knee. Each group will need to choose a facilitator, who will guide her group through the entire Sacred Story exercise. We will remain in quiet reflection and prayer until all of the groups are finished. (STOP) ♥

Imagine This!
Note: The small group facilitator begins reading here.

Turn in your journal to page 29, "Imagine This! Sacred Story Bible Study: House Cleaning." (STOP) In this exercise we will read the Sacred Story three times. After each reading, we will be instructed to close our eyes and use our imaginations to discover the story's meaning for us.

First I will quickly read all the way through the step-by-step directions aloud. (STOP)

Now I will read the directions slowly a second time, pausing at each step as indicated and appropriate so that we may work through the process together.

Note: Follow the directions on pages 29–31 in your journal to com-plete the study. When finished, return quietly to the larger circle and fast from speech until everyone has completed the study. (STOP) ♥

A Hearty Goodbye

Each of us has carried a message from the heart since our last gath-ering. We now are invited to give our hearts away. Give your heart-word to someone in the group, perhaps a person you sense could use this word. If you forgot your heart, don't panic. Simply tell the other person the word so that she may write it in her journal at the bottom of page 27. If you do not receive a word from another person, you are invited to pick a new word from the heart-words on pages 26–27 of your journal.**STOP**

Let us prepare to leave by reading aloud together this lighthearted prayer:**STOP**

> **Big-hearted God,**
> **We are a gathering of women with**
> > **hopeful hearts,**
> > **broken hearts,**
> > **lonely hearts,**
> > **fragile hearts,**
> > **empty hearts,**
> > **longing hearts,**
> > **aching hearts.**
>
> **But, if truth be told (and we promise to be truth tellers),**
> **We also are women who are**
> > **happy-hearted,**
> > **open-hearted,**
> > **whole-hearted,**
> > **cheerful-hearted,**
> > **true-hearted.**
>
> **Our hearts are full of the joy**
> > **that only you can give,**
> > **and that we must receive for ourselves.**
>
> **May our lives be a heart-song for you. Amen.**

Gathering 3 will take place on *(date/s)* at *(time/s and place/s)*. *Note: If you are using the multiple groups format, explain that participants may attend any scheduled gathering. If the group needs to discuss meeting dates, times, and places, do so now.* **STOP** ♥

Note: The person facilitating the following breathing exercise may not be able to participate fully. Remember to pause at least ten seconds or longer at each **STOP**.

Before we leave, place your feet flat on the floor.🛑 Remove everything from your lap and hands.🛑 Take a long, deep breath and hold it for a count of ten. 🛑 Now blow it out. 🛑 When everyone has opened her eyes, we will stand.🛑

Today I light a special taper candle.🛑 As we pass it from person to person, we show the bond that is growing among us as we share our light, wisdom, and strength with one another. Turn to the person standing to your right and, as you hand her the candle, say:

Go, knowing you are loved. 🛑

Remember to take off your nametag and place it on the focus center as you leave. As I extinguish the candle, go in God's love. 🛑

Gathering 3

Heartbeat

Note: Break free from the hectic pace of everyday life with music. As women gather, play selections from any of the three categories included in the "Bibliography of Suggested Music"—"Meditative," "Music for Movement," and "Sing-along." See the "Appendix," pages 200–03. Or you may choose other appropriate songs.

Circle of Hearts

Note: One woman begins the gathering by reading the following aloud to the group. Remember to read slowly, leaving space for silence. For more detailed reminders on how to open and conduct a Heart to Heart *gathering, refer to "Getting Started," pages 28–32.*

Welcome to this third gathering of *Heart to Heart*. We begin, as we have in our first two gatherings, with rituals. The hospitalities we extend and the trust that is developing among us are subtle rituals in which we help create a safe space for one another. You may say "pass" anytime you do not wish to participate, and the role of facilitator will move to the woman on your right.

If we have not already done so, let us circle our chairs around a central table—our focus center. **STOP** Now I will take the articles for our gathering from the supply box and arrange them on the focus center: a cloth covering, a candle and matches (or a lighter), a heart-shaped box, a hand-sized heart, nametags, a wide-edged felt-tip pen, a bell, and a bowl of potpourri. **STOP**

As we have done at our previous gatherings, let us now receive our nametags from one another. Remember, allow another member of the gathering to pin your nametag on you. When everyone finishes, we will proceed. (STOP)

Heartbeat

Note: You may wish to play some quiet background music during "Heartwarmers." Choose selections from the "Meditative" category on page 201 in the "Bibliography of Suggested Music," or choose other appropriate songs.

Heartwarmers

I am moving to light the candle on our focus center to mark the beginning of our gathering. (STOP) As I light this candle, join me in saying these words from our teacher, Jesus. Repeat each line aloud after me: (STOP)

Do not worry about your life, (STOP)
   what you will eat or what you will drink, (STOP)
   or about your body, what you will wear. (STOP)

Is not life more than food, (STOP)
   and the body more than clothing? (STOP)

But strive first for the kingdom of God (STOP)
   and his righteousness, (STOP)
   and all these things (STOP)
   will be given to you as well. (STOP) ♥
                                    —*Matthew 6:25b, c, 33*

Note: The person facilitating may not be able to participate fully in the following body prayer ritual. Pause at least ten seconds or longer at each (STOP) .

Before we continue, let's stop and consider: Have we been rushing all day? Perhaps our whole lives? Let's take a moment now to relax, to

73

slow our physical selves, and to pray. As we enter into this time of prayer, let us know that debating endless hours over how to do a prayer ritual or discussing its deeper meaning is not always necessary. Often it is best to jump right in and do prayer—see how prayer works and feels. It is not always true that ritual must represent something. Sometimes the reality works the other way. The meaning develops out of the doing.

First Corinthians, chapter 6, of the Sacred Scriptures reads: "Therefore glorify God in your body." Our outward posture often reflects our inward state. The body, mind, and spirit are inseparable. This body prayer is called "Palms Up, Palms Down."

Sit comfortably. **STOP** Put aside anything in your hands and lap. **STOP** Place your feet flat on the floor. **STOP** Close your eyes. **STOP** Begin by placing your palms down as a symbolic indication of your desire to turn over any concerns you may have to God. Whatever it is that weighs you down, release it. *Note: Pause one to two minutes.* **STOP**

Now, turn your palms up as a symbol of your desire to receive from the Lord. **STOP** Silently name what you need. *Note: Pause one to two minutes.* **STOP**

Spend the next two minutes remaining in silence. Do not relinquish anything or ask anything. Be still in your heart, and sit in God's presence. Allow the Lord to speak to you. *Note: Pause two minutes.* **STOP**

Now, as you are ready, return your attention to the room and open your eyes. When everyone's eyes are open, we will continue. **STOP** ♥

A prayer ritual may have many layers of meaning to different people, and each woman relates to God in her own way. Some ways of "being in the presence of God" work for some individuals and groups but not for others. Because prayer affects different people in different ways, let's take a moment to debrief. As we talk about what happened, we are more able to integrate it into our lives. *Note: Talk together for several minutes about the body prayer ritual you have just experienced.* **STOP** ♥

Heartbeat

Note: Choose a song from the "Sing-along" category on pages 202–03 in the "Bibliography of Suggested Music," or another song, and be prepared to play and/or sing the selection when indicated.

We claim this time as special and this place as holy. We learn about

74

life by taking time to reflect on our experiences. As we stop to look at our lives—at who we are—we begin to see the sacred within our lives and within ourselves. Listen to this song; sing along if you wish. *Note: Play the song now.* 🛑

Let us pause for prayer. Pray aloud with me. 🛑

> **Spirit of Wisdom,**
> > **Teach us to take time to celebrate one another.**
> **Spirit of Truth,**
> > **Help us to balance our lives between reflection and action.**
> > > > > > **Amen. ♥**

From the Heart Journal: A Personal Prayer Journal for Women

The simple act of lighting a candle is a ritual that defines sacred time. We have many rituals in our lives. Rituals, often called traditions, spring up especially during holidays. They are the special touches and occasions, unique to us, that we celebrate or remember. Rituals provide us the opportunity to say, "This is who we are; this is our special way of celebrating." In a moment we will think about rituals that are important to you. ♥

Now turn in your journal to pages 32 and 33, "Rituals and Celebrations Are Important." 🛑 We will fast from speech as we record our reflections in our journals. When we finish, we will go around the circle and read what we have written. Remember, you will be asked to share only as you are comfortable. Beginning now, you have two minutes to write. I will tell you when time is up. *Note: Ring the bell when two minutes have expired.* 🛑

You've Got to Have Heart

Time is up. I am moving to take the hand-sized heart from the focus center. 🛑 As we have done before, we will pass the heart around the circle as we share. When the heart comes to you, it is your turn to share. When you are finished, pass the heart to the woman on your right. We will continue in this manner until everyone has had the opportunity to share. If anyone does not wish to share, she simply passes the heart. When we are finished, we will return the heart to the focus center. Since I am holding the heart, I will start by sharing one of the rituals I wrote about. _Note: After you have shared, pass the heart to the woman on your right. When all others in the circle who wish to share have done so and the heart has made its way back to you, return it to the focus center._ 🛑 ♥

A Heart-Centered Story

The Quest of the Woman in Search of Her Heart

Chapter 3

In Chapter 1 of our story, we met Questa, the woman who lost her heart. Then, in Chapter 2, we traveled with her far into the country to the door of a wise woman named Sage. Chapter 2 ended with Sage asking Questa, "Do you want to find your heart?" She then told Questa that Questa herself is the only one who knows the way back to her heart. As Chapter 3 opens, Sage has just suggested that Questa go for a walk to sort out her thoughts. As you continue the story, remember to read slowly and thoughtfully.

Questa is thankful for Sage's suggestion that she take a walk; the walk helps clear Questa's head. _This Sage is clueless,_ thinks the woman without a heart. Surely Sage is off in "la-la land." "Talk more," Sage had said. About what?

As she returns, Questa finds Sage on the sun porch, reading. "Look," Questa says, "all these introspective questions can wait. I've got immediate problems. I've got to get home and return to my work." ♥

Sage stops reading and peers over the rim of her glasses. "That's your problem," she says.

Questa is too tired for this game. She begins to pull on a hangnail. The next line tumbles out in exasperation: "What in the world are you talking about?" Questa can't believe she just said that. *How could I be so rude?* she silently chides herself, unable to hide her embarrassment. ♥

Sage looks at Questa and says, "I'm talking about you." Her look is one of care, as one would give a hurt child. "You may leave," she continues. "Go back to pretending you're all together. You are very good at that. No one will ever know who you really are—or aren't. Besides, you've got it more together than many women." ♥

Questa is feeling better now. This stranger is beginning to understand. It will all work out. Her heart will return in due time. In the meantime, she'll just keep herself busy.

Sage laughs gently. *At her?* Questa wonders.

"I'm sorry," Questa says.

"Why are you apologizing?" asks Sage. ♥

Sage's question hits a soft spot within Questa. *Why am I apologizing?* Questa wonders. It is an old habit. When she feels vulnerable, she plays the little girl. Lowering her volume and slowing her speech, she places herself at the other's mercy to stave off the possible attack.

"Maybe you need to stop trying so hard," says Sage. "Consider instead a new way: a journey back to your heart, your true home—back to find the compassion of which you yourself spoke. You're always busy, but never fulfilled. Your hours are full, but your life is empty." ♥

Questa wants to protest, but she is exhausted. For the woman without a heart, the price of remaining numb is too high, and it is growing higher every day. Images of the Stepford wives spring to mind—suburban robotic Barbie dolls living the life of domestic perfectionism. The effect is simultaneously hilarious, scary, and even sad—a melancholy parable about the loss of one's soul.

Just then Questa feels a fluttering in her chest. A coincidence? She knows she is stressed out. It must be the anxiety getting to her. ♥

"This isn't what you expected?" Sage asks.

This mysterious wise one is right. This isn't what Questa has come for. Not at all. "You seem to know everything about me," Questa admits, feeling relief and shame at the same time.

Sage pours Questa more coffee. "You have been in this situation before, haven't you?" It is more of a statement than a question.

"Yes, of course," says Questa.

"Do you learn from hard times?" Sage inquires. "From your choices?"

Questa tries to review the many choices she's made through the years, times when she has taken responsibility for her decisions. To marry or remain single. To have a child or not. To diet or keep eating. To go to school or work. To take this job or pursue that career. To speak or remain silent. To risk or play it safe. She gives up. "Sometimes," she finally answers. ♥

Sage tells her a story. She explains that it is an "Autobiography in Five Short Chapters."

CHAPTER ONE

I walk down the street.
> There is a deep hole in the sidewalk.
> I fall in.
> I am lost. . . I am helpless.
> It isn't my fault.
It takes forever to find a way out.

CHAPTER TWO

I walk down the same street.
> There is a deep hole in the sidewalk.
> I pretend I don't see it.
> I fall in again.
I can't believe I am in this same place.
> But it isn't my fault.
It still takes a long time to get out. ♥

CHAPTER THREE

I walk down the same street.
There is a deep hole in the sidewalk.
I see it is there.
I still fall in . . . it's a habit . . . but,
my eyes are open.
I know where I am.
It is my fault.
I get out immediately. ♥

CHAPTER FOUR

I walk down the same street.
There is a deep hole in the sidewalk.
I walk around it. ♥

CHAPTER FIVE

I walk down another street. ♥ *

"So you're saying that if I don't like my choices, perhaps I need to find a new street?" asks Questa.

Sage responds in her matter-of-fact voice: "Learning to take responsibility for ourselves is a spiritual process. Sometimes that means making a change. Sometimes it means that we 'walk down another street.' Life is full of choices. We need to make our choices and take responsibility for them." There is a lengthy pause. "Shall we move on?" Sage asks. ♥

Move on to what? Questa wonders. *Aimless puzzling stories?* Still, perhaps Sage knows more about the whereabouts of her heart than she is saying. "Maybe. I'm not sure," Questa responds.

"Take some time to think about it," Sage suggests. "Another walk, perhaps? But you may want to look down the street first and note where the holes are. We can talk more when you get back." *To be continued.* . . . ♥

*From *There's a Hole in My Sidewalk: The Romance of Self-Discovery,* by Portia Nelson. Copyright © 1993 by Portia Nelson. Published by Beyond Words Publishing, Inc. Used by permission.

Sacred Story Bible Study

Note: If this is a thirty-minute gathering, or if your group will not be doing the Bible study together for another reason, move on to the next section. Take some time this week to read and reflect on the Sacred Story.

Devotional reading of the Scripture has always been a wellspring of the spiritual life. As we open ourselves to God's works through the Scripture, we invite the Holy Spirit to pray in us. Dorotheus of Gaza, who lived during the sixth century, wrote, "Such is the nature of love, the nearer we draw to God in love, the more we are united together by love for our neighbor; and the greater our union with our neighbor, the greater our union with God." Through the Sacred Stories, God draws us into the divine self. ♥

So far in *Heart to Heart*, we have used a group method of spiritual reading called *lectio divina,* which means "divine reading." In this gathering, we will use a new form of this devotional reading method called "Praying the Scripture." This method will help us dive under the surface of the words to find their deeper meaning.

If there are more than five women in our full group, we will divide into small circles of three to five by choosing women whom we know the least. We will space our groups around the room and circle our chairs so that we are sitting knee to knee. Each group will need to choose a facilitator, who will guide her group through the entire Sacred Story exercise. We will remain in quiet reflection and prayer until all of the groups are finished. 🛑 ♥

Praying the Scripture

Note: The small group facilitator begins reading here.

Turn in your journal to page 34, "Praying the Scripture Sacred Story Bible Study: Keepin' On." First, I will read through the instructions, which appear in bold print. 🛑 Now, as I begin reading at Step 1 a second time, I will read all the words, including the wise words of Madame Jeanne Guyon, which appear in italics. Madame Guyon was a Christian woman who lived in France from 1648 to 1717. Her instructions on Scripture and prayer are as relevant today as they were over 280 years ago. After reading each segment, I will pause so that we may work through the process together. 🛑

*Note: Follow the directions on pages 34–36 in your journal to com-
plete the study. When finished, return quietly to the larger circle and
fast from speech until everyone has completed the study.* (STOP) ♥

From the Heart Journal:
A Personal Prayer Journal for Women

Now turn in your journal to pages 37–39, "Holes in My Sidewalk."
(STOP) During the next ten minutes, we will fast from speech and write in
our journals. We will stop all talk from this moment until we regroup.
If you are not used to solitude, this ten minutes may seem like a life-
time. Remember, learning comes as you observe your feelings and
reactions. Take this opportunity to become aware of what you are feeling in this time of solitude, this time apart. Ask yourself: "What does
this experience tell me about myself?"

You are invited to find a quiet space to claim as your own. You may
want to move to another part of the room, another room, or outside to
write. I will let you know when time is up by ringing the bell. *Note:
Ring the bell when ten minutes have expired.* (STOP)

Let us break our period of silence with a prayer. Pray with me: (STOP)

God, we open our hearts to a new awareness
   of the choices we make and the streets we take.
We need insight and courage to miss the holes,
   and maybe even to walk down a new street. Amen. ♥

You've Got to Have Heart

If time permits, each of us will turn now to another person in the circle and share one of the "holes" in our street. As we do this, we will
ask ourselves, "What new choice can I make this week?" *Note: If you
are within five minutes of the agreed-upon ending time, do not share
at this time. Instead, announce that those who wish may remain after
the formal goodbye and share with another person. Then move on to
the next section.* (STOP)

Heartbeat

Note: After you have attended to scheduling matters as directed in "A Hearty Goodbye," play quiet, gentle music in the background during the closing prayer ritual. Choose from the "Meditative" category on page 201 in the "Bibliography of Suggested Music," or choose other appropriate songs.

A Hearty Goodbye

Gathering 4 will take place on *(date/s)* at *(time/s and place/s). Note: If you are using the multiple groups format, explain that participants may attend any scheduled gathering. If the group needs to discuss meeting dates, times, and places, do so now.* **STOP**

Note: The person facilitating the following prayer ritual may not be able to participate fully. Pause at least ten seconds or longer at each **STOP** .

Before we leave, put down everything you are holding. **STOP** Plant your feet flat on the floor. **STOP** Close your eyes and take a long, deep breath. **STOP** Hold it for a count of ten. **STOP** Now blow it out. **STOP** When everyone has opened her eyes, we will stand. **STOP** ♥

Today, I pass a fragrant basket of potpourri around the circle. As we pass this incense from person to person, I invite you to run your fingers through the sweet smells. As you share in the aroma of Christ, hear these words from the Psalms. . . . *Note: As the music continues playing, slowly read the following poem until the potpourri has traveled completely around the circle.* **STOP**

"I call upon you, O Lord; come quickly to me;
   give ear to my voice when I call to you.
Let my prayer be counted as incense before you,
   and the lifting up of my hands as an evening sacrifice."

—*Psalm 141:1-2*

As we close, let us join hands. **STOP** Close your eyes and take a long, deep breath. **STOP** Hold it for a count of ten. **STOP** Now blow it out. **STOP**

When everyone has opened her eyes, we will continue. **STOP** Now, with hands still joined, lift them toward the center as a prayer of thanksgiving to God. **STOP** Repeat after me: **STOP**

We are the beloved of God. STOP
Amen! STOP

Remember to take off your nametag and place it on the focus center as you leave. As I extinguish the candle, go in God's love. **STOP**

Gathering 4

Heartbeat

Note: Choose music that tickles your fancy and play it as you reconnect, and gather into a circle before your starting time. See the "Bibliography of Suggested Music," pages 200–03, or choose other appropriate songs.

Circle of Hearts

Note: One woman begins the gathering by reading the following aloud to the group. Remember to read slowly, allowing time for reflection as appropriate. For more detailed reminders on how to open and conduct a Heart to Heart gathering, refer to "Getting Started," pages 28–32.

Let's congratulate ourselves for taking time in our busy lives to continue this journey with one another. It's hard to take time to do spiritual work for ourselves, but here we are again!

If we have not already done so, let us circle our chairs around a central table—our focus center. **STOP** Now I will take the articles for our gathering from the supply box and arrange them on the focus center: a cloth covering, a candle and matches (or a lighter), a cloth napkin, a heart-shaped box, a hand-sized heart, nametags, a wide-edged felt-tip pen, a bell, a blessing cup, and a bottle of chilled, flavored water. **STOP**

Every woman is encouraged to participate fully, but you may say

"Pass" anytime you do not wish to read or participate. Now, choose a nametag and pin it on the woman it names. Remember, do not take your own nametag. When everyone has completed this task and returned to her seat, we will continue. (STOP)

Heartbeat

Note: You may wish to play some quiet background music during "Heartwarmers." Choose selections from the "Meditative" category on page 201 in the "Bibliography of Suggested Music," or other appropriate songs.

Heartwarmers

As I move to light the candle on the focus center, we acknowledge this special place *just for us*—a place where we may become better acquainted with the sacred self that enlivens us; a place where we may grow to understand who we are and whom God intends us to be. We know that we are taking time to do important spiritual work. (STOP) ♥

Note: The person facilitating the following prayer ritual may not be able to participate fully. Remember to pause for at least ten seconds at each (STOP).

Assume a relaxed position. (STOP) Place your feet flat on the floor. (STOP) Put down everything in your hands and lap. (STOP) Hold your hands palms up in your lap. (STOP) Now take three deep breaths—breathing the way you've learned in previous gatherings—to calm yourself and acknowledge the presence of God. You may focus on the candlelight or close your eyes. When we have taken our three deep breaths, we will proceed. (STOP)

We need to take care not to distort this spiritual work—and these gatherings—into another form of "self-improvement." Self-improvement articles and books imply that there is something terribly wrong with us. They make us dwell on our "warts" instead of our "beauty marks." On the other hand, the work of the Spirit is based on God's love for us. God tells us we can stop trying to live up to magazine and movie standards. We can feel OK as we are, knowing that God is working through us. ♥

In these opening minutes, let's pause for prayer. Pray aloud with me: (STOP)

> **God, you know us, beauty marks and all.**
> **Help us to stop trying to live up to others' expectations**
> **and to live only in your will for our lives. Amen.** ♥

Spiritual work is not done at a brisk pace. Deep spiritual work happens as we set time aside for that purpose. The Spirit travels at an unhurried tempo. Repeat after me the words of our teacher, Jesus: (STOP)

> **"The eye is the lamp of the body.** (STOP)
> **So, if your eye is healthy,** (STOP)
> **your whole body will be full of light;** (STOP)
> **but if your eye is unhealthy,**
> **your whole body will be full of darkness."** (STOP)
> —*Matthew 6:22-23*

We need to be careful lest we make the mistake of doing spiritual work in a way that does not have spiritual light. ♥

From the Heart Journal:
A Personal Prayer Journal for Women

Now turn in your journal to pages 40–41, "Heart-Centered Words for My Life." (STOP) Choose words that describe you from page 40 and write them in the heart on page 41. You also may use words that are not listed. Complete as much as you can in the next three minutes. After three minutes, we will share what we have written. I will let you know when time is up. *Note: Ring the bell after three minutes.* (STOP)

You've Got to Have Heart

Time's up. I am moving to take the hand-sized heart from the focus center. **STOP** As we have done before, we will pass the heart around the circle as we share. When the heart comes to you, it is your turn to share three of the words you wrote in your heart. When you are finished, pass the heart to the woman on your right. We will continue in this manner until everyone has had the opportunity to share. Remember, share only as you are comfortable. If you do not wish to share, simply pass the heart. When we are finished, we will return the heart to the focus center. Since I am holding the heart, I will begin by sharing three words I have chosen to describe myself. _Note: After you share, pass the heart to the woman on your right. When all others in the circle who wish to share have done so and the heart has made its way back to you, return it to the focus center._ **STOP** ♥

A Heart-Centered Story

The Quest of the Woman in Search of Her Heart

Chapter 4

In Chapter 3, Questa, the woman without a heart, began to see that the cost of remaining numb had become too high. Sage told her a story about a woman who repeatedly fell into holes until one day she made a different choice and took a new course. Sensing Questa's growing frustration, Sage suggested she take another walk to sort out her feelings. Chapter 4 begins with Questa returning from her walk. As you continue the story, remember to read slowly and thoughtfully.

The woman without a heart returns from her walk, weary, and goes to bed. She awakens the next morning to find the house and garden empty. She finds some fruit on the kitchen counter and eats it. She lives the morning in solitude with only the sounds of singing birds and the distant splashing of a fountain. It doesn't get any better than this, she thinks. Yet she feels, not the pleasure one might expect on such a perfect day, but a lingering sense of sadness. She can't remember her last morning of leisure. *I should do this more often,* she thinks. *But I have too much to do.* ♥

The sounds, sights, and smells of nature heighten Questa's sense of connectedness to the earth. They touch her heart. *Heart?* She almost thinks she heard a beat last night as she closed her eyes and drifted off to sleep. "A journey back to her heart," Sage had said. How about a map for this trip? She'll ask Sage for one. ♥

Sage returns and suggests they go for a walk. "There is no map," Sage tells Questa when she asks for one. "You find your heart by opening yourself to receive it. As you open yourself, you will find a sanctuary where you may grow. You will discover integrity and calling in your work. You will reclaim the faith that gives your life passion, purpose, and direction. You will live only what is God's will for your life." ♥

"And what is God's will for my life?" Questa asks.

Sage responds warmly, "Living God's will means being in tune with the heart of God. Finding God's will and purpose for our lives is not some mysterious path that only the most pious may walk. Living in God's will is not choosing between 'door number one' or 'door number two'—or believing that only one of the doors is truly God's path for us. It is not believing that there is one perfect mate or vocation or calling. It is not believing that if we don't find the ultimate it, our life, and our heart, will be forever out of rhythm." Sage pauses, as if contemplating what to say next. ♥

As she walks off the main road, through some bushes, Sage leads Questa to a less-traveled side path. Normally Questa shies away from such divergence, but since Sage seems to know where she is going, Questa follows.

Sage continues, "Living in God's will means that we live our lives—with whatever choices we make or whatever twists and turns we find along our path—in touch with the heart of God. We open ourselves each day in a fresh way, knowing that God gives us what we need for the day." ♥

The path continues to narrow. The women now pick their way though overhanging vines and branches. *Where is Sage taking me?* Questa wonders. "Stop!" she suddenly demands. Sage stops and turns toward her.

"Look, I didn't come here for a sermon," Questa says to Sage. "I just want my heart back. I am hoping for some concrete advice. I like 'to do' lists. I need specific directions." ♥

Sage answers, "God's will and Spirit defy strict definition. To try to pin things down hampers the Spirit's work. To proceed in your accustomed way turns life into an intellectual exercise, neglecting the heart."

Sage leads Questa to a fallen tree where there is room for them both to sit. "Living in God's will does not hinge on a role, title, or position you undertake," Sage continues. "It cannot be measured by success or failure as defined by the world. Mary the mother of Jesus was the supreme example of a woman in tune with the heart of God. She sang,

'My soul magnifies the Lord, my spirit rejoices in God my Savior.' Like Mary, we can joyfully live in God's will." ♥

The women sit in silence for a time.

Then Sage bends close to Questa's ear and whispers, "How could I possibly give you directions to your own heart?"

"I came to you because you're a psychologist. Aren't you?" asks Questa. She searches for a clue as to why Sage talks in such mystical terms.

"No," says Sage.

"A philosopher?" Questa quizzes.

"No. At least, not professionally," says Sage.

"Some kind of church lady?" Questa explores.

Sage laughs. "Giving 'church chats'? Never." There is a long pause. Then Sage asks, "Does the journey scare you?"

"Yes," Questa responds sincerely. "And it confuses me." ♥

Sage smiles and tells Questa a story:

Jesus, tired out by his journey, was sitting by Jacob's well. It was about noon. A Samaritan woman came to draw water, and Jesus said to her, "Give me a drink." (His disciples had gone to the city to buy food.)

The Samaritan woman said to him, "How is it that you, a Jew, ask a drink of me, a woman of Samaria?" (Jews do not share things in common with Samaritans.)

Jesus answered her, "If you knew the gift of God, and who it is that is saying to you, 'Give me a drink,' you would have asked him, and he would have given you living water."

The woman said to him, "Sir, you have no bucket, and the well is deep. Where do you get that living water? Are you greater than our ancestor Jacob, who gave us the well and with his sons and his flocks drank from it?"

Jesus said to her, "Everyone who drinks of this water will be thirsty again, but those who drink of the water that I will give them will never be thirsty. The water that I will give will become in them a spring of water gushing up to eternal life."

The woman said to him, "Sir, give me this water, so that I may never be thirsty or have to keep coming here to draw water" (John 4:7-15). ♥

The woman without a heart sees her own life reflected in this ancient tale from Scripture. She is like the woman in the story—thirsty. "You're talking about me?" Questa asks.

"Do you think so?" asks Sage.

The two women continue up the path. ♥

"A journey to the heart goes through territory that many before you have walked. You do not go alone," says Sage.

"You mean like Mary and the woman who got a spiritual drink from Jesus?" asks Questa.

Silence. A chipmunk with its cheeks filled with nuts scampers across the path. It knows where it is going. Why doesn't she?

"Where do I begin?" Questa asks.

"Where you are," Sage replies.

"I'm not sure where I am anymore," Questa responds.

"That's a good beginning," says Sage.

"A good beginning for what?" asks Questa.

"For your journey."

To be continued. . . . ♥

Heartbeat

Note: Choose a selection from the "Sing-along" category on pages 202–03 in the "Bibliography of Suggested Music"—or another song— and sing along!

Sacred Story Bible Study

Note: If this is a thirty-minute gathering, or if your group will not be doing the Bible study together for another reason, move on to the journaling exercise on page 92. Take some time this week to read and reflect on the Sacred Story.

The book *Circle of Hearts: A Woman's Guide to Creating Your Own Spirituality Group* says this about reading the Sacred Stories:

> We sit and read a gospel text for the umpteenth time when, finally, its words are able to penetrate our skulls. There, squarely in front of us, within that page of words, sits our lives. We are the Samaritan at the well, Mary washing Jesus' feet, and the unnamed bent-over woman healed by Jesus. Through their stories we are empowered to open our mouths and put into words, perhaps for the first time, our own precarious stories of faith. ♥
>
> Interacting with biblical stories naturally leads to talking about our personal stories. And we love to talk! Yet, as we draw on Scripture to make sense of our lives, this talk is not frivolous but meaningful. Sharing our journeys can be a source of wisdom and insight for ourselves as well as those within earshot. When we are the listener, we get to eavesdrop on another's experiences; and suddenly we don't feel quite as alone in our own feelings and realities.* ♥

So far in *Heart to Heart* we have used three methods of "Sacred Story Bible Study." At this gathering, we will use the fourth and final method,

---

*From chapter 1, *Circle of Hearts*, by Patricia D. Brown; copyright 1998 by Spiritworks. Available from the Florida Conference Council on Ministries of The United Methodist Church.

called "Responsive Listening." This oral tradition Bible study leads us in reading the Scripture together three times. After each reading, we aloud God's will for our lives. This approach helps us open ourselves to hear God's Word anew and apply it to our hearts and lives. Through the responsive listening method, Bible stories meet us in our own life stories. These stories allow us to gain insight and hear God's voice as we listen to what others have to share.

If there are more than five women in our full group, we will divide into small circles of three to five by choosing women whom we know the least. We will space our groups around the room and circle our chairs so that we are sitting knee to knee. Each group will need to choose a facilitator, who will guide her group through the entire Sacred Story exercise. We will remain in quiet reflection and prayer until all of the groups are finished. 🛑 ♥

Responsive Listening

Note: The small group facilitator begins reading here.

Turn in your journal to page 42, "Responsive Listening Sacred Story Bible Study: Thirsty." I will read through the step-by-step directions aloud. 🛑

Now I will read the directions a second time, pausing at each step so that we may work through the process together. 🛑

Note: Follow the directions on pages 42–45 in your journal to complete the study. When finished, return quietly to the larger circle and fast from speech until everyone has completed the study. 🛑 ♥

Heartbeat

Note: Choose a song to sing together or to listen to during a time of quiet meditation before moving on to the journaling exercise. See the "Sing-along" selections on pages 202–03 in the "Bibliography of Suggested Music," or choose a favorite song of your group.

From the Heart Journal:
A Personal Prayer Journal for Women

Now we will take ten minutes to fast from speech. This means we will stop all talk from the moment we begin journaling until time is up.

Turn in your journal to pages 46 and 47, "Gather a Cloud of Witnesses." **STOP** Sage reminds the woman searching for her heart that "a journey to the heart goes through territory that many before you have walked. You do not go alone." Who are the sages, crones, and wise ones—women, both living and dead—in your life? Celebrate them for the next ten minutes by thinking about them and writing their names in the spaces provided in your journal.

I invite you now to find a quiet space to claim as your own. You may want to move to another part of the room, another room, or outside to write. I will let you know when time is up by ringing the bell. We then will come back together and break our silence with sharing and prayer. _Note: Ring the bell after ten minutes._ **STOP** ♥

You've Got to Have Heart

I am moving to take the hand-sized heart from the focus center. **STOP** As we have done before, we will pass the heart around the circle as we share. When the heart comes to you, it is your turn to share one of your "clouds of witnesses." When you are finished, pass the heart to the woman on your right. We will continue in this manner until everyone has had the opportunity to share. If anyone does not wish to share, she simply passes the heart. When we are finished, we will return the heart to the focus center. Since I am holding the heart, I will share first. _Note: If it is too close to the agreed-upon ending time, skip ahead to the prayer and then move on to the next section. Please remain faithful to the time schedule you agreed upon at the start of your gatherings. Those who wish to remain after the formal goodbye to share with others may do so. If you have time for sharing, pass the heart around the_ *circle until everyone who wishes to share has done so. When the heart makes its way back to you, return it to the focus center.* 🛑 ♥

Now let us pause for prayer. In this prayer you are invited to name aloud women who, in life or in death, continue to bring you courage and strength. Let us stand and pray together: 🛑

God, you are so amazing. You have brought us together, and we feel

your presence with us. Yet we do not stand here alone. There is a cloud of witnesses surrounding us who, like Mary and the woman of Samaria, stand with us even now. We name them aloud now.

Note: Now, one at a time, say the names of women who bring you courage and strength. 🛑

We thank you for the witness of these women whose stories make us strong. Amen. ♥

Heartbeat

Note: Choose gentle background music from the "Meditative" selections found on page 201 of the "Bibliography of Suggested Music," or choose another song. Begin playing the music after you have made your arrangements for Gathering 5.

A Hearty Goodbye

Gathering 5 will take place on *(date/s)* at *(time/s and place/s). Note: If you are using the multiple groups format, explain that participants may attend any scheduled gathering. If the group needs to discuss meeting dates, times, and places, do so now.* 🛑

Note: Move to the focus center and pour some of the chilled, flavored water into the blessing cup. As you return to your place in the circle, take the blessing cup and cloth napkin with you. Then continue. **STOP** Just as Jesus shared a drink of water with the Samaritan woman, his new friend, so also we share this blessing cup. In our closing prayer ritual, we ask God to bless this cup of friendship. We ask God to give us the compassion and mercy we need to be loving friends.

I invite you to take a drink of water from the blessing cup, wipe it with the cloth napkin, and pass it to the next woman. Or you may simply hold the cup in prayerful reflection for a moment and then pass it on. *Note: Take a drink from the blessing cup, wipe it with the cloth napkin, and pass both items to the woman on your right. When the cup and napkin have made their way around the circle, continue.* **STOP**

Pray aloud with me. **STOP**

> **We thank you, God, for the gift of friendship.**
> **May we always be united in loving community.**
> **We ask this in the name of Jesus,**
> **the one who gives living water. Amen. ♥**

Note: The person facilitating the following relaxation exercise may not be able to participate fully. Pause at least ten seconds or more at each **STOP** .

As we prepare to leave, put everything out of your hands and lap. **STOP** Place your feet flat on the floor. **STOP** Close your eyes and take a long, deep breath. **STOP** Hold it for a count of ten. **STOP** Now, blow it out. **STOP** When everyone has opened her eyes, we will stand. **STOP**

Remember to take off your nametag and place it on the focus center as you leave. As I extinguish the candle, go in God's love. **STOP**

Gathering 5

Heartbeat

Note: The power of music will help your group "settle in" with one another. To set the stage for your gathering, make selections from the "Meditative," "Music for Movement," or "Sing-along" categories in the "Bibliography of Suggested Music." See pages 200–03 in the "Appendix." Or choose other appropriate songs. Enjoy!

Circle of Hearts

Note: One woman begins the gathering by reading the following aloud to the group. Remember to read at an unhurried pace, allowing time for silence. For more detailed reminders on how to open and conduct a Heart to Heart *gathering, refer to "Getting Started," pages 28–32.*

Welcome to *Heart to Heart*. We begin our fifth gathering, as we have our previous gatherings, with a heart-centered ritual. If we have not already done so, let us circle our chairs around a central table—our focus center.

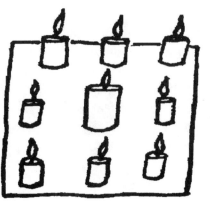

STOP Now I will take the articles for our gathering from the supply box and arrange them on the focus center: a cloth covering, a candle and matches (or a lighter), a heart-shaped box, a hand-sized heart, nametags, a wide-edged felt-tip pen, a bell, and small candles—one for each of us—to be placed in a circular formation around the center candle.(STOP) Remember, anytime anyone does not wish to participate, she simply says "Pass," and the role of facilitator moves to the next woman. ♥

Let us begin by praying aloud together:(STOP)

God, since you are always with us, we never despair.
We rejoice in your continual healing in our lives. Amen.

Now choose a nametag and pin it on the woman it names. When everyone finishes, we will proceed. (STOP) ♥

Heartbeat

Note: Choose meditative music to play during "Heartwarmers." See the listing on page 201 in the "Bibliography of Suggested Music," or choose another song.(STOP)

Heartwarmers

I light the candle on our focus center to symbolize the Holy Spirit, who dwells within each of us. (STOP) We share the Spirit's light, strength, and wisdom with one another in our gatherings.

Hear now these words from our teacher, Jesus. Repeat each line after me:(STOP)

"Can any of you by worrying (STOP)
add a single hour to your span of life? (STOP)
Consider the lilies of the field, how they grow; (STOP)
they neither toil nor spin, (STOP)
So do not worry about tomorrow, (STOP)
for tomorrow will bring worries of its own. (STOP)
Today's trouble is enough for today." (STOP)
—*Matthew 6:27-28, 34*

Note: The person facilitating the following prayer ritual may not be able to participate fully. Remember to pause at least ten seconds or more at each (STOP) .

Prayer rituals are a bridge between the inner and outer worlds, reconnecting us to a deeper reality. Let us begin by calming our hearts as we claim this special place and time.

Place your feet flat on the floor. **(STOP)** Put everything out of your lap and hands. **(STOP)** Close your eyes. **(STOP)** Pull your shoulders down from your ears. **(STOP)** Hold this position for a count of five; then release. **(STOP)** Now pull your shoulders up toward your ears. **(STOP)** Hold this position for a count of five; then release. **(STOP)** Take three relaxing, deep breaths as you sit in God's presence with friends. Breathe in to the count of ten and exhale to the count of twelve. **(STOP)** When all eyes are open, we will continue. **(STOP)**

Today there are individual candles on the focus center, one for each of us. One at a time, let us take a candle from the table, return to our seat, place our feet flat on the floor, and hold our candle in our lap. **(STOP)**

Silently pray for the grace to love all people with deep compassion. Close your eyes and picture yourself living nonjudgmentally toward yourself, thereby having the compassion to love others with the same mercy. We will pause for one minute. *Note: Continue reading after one minute.* **(STOP)**

Now, form your thoughts into a prayer. We will pause for one minute. *Note: Continue reading after one minute.* **(STOP)**

As you offer up your silent prayer, move to the focus center, light your candle from the center candle, and place your lighted candle on the table as a reminder of the inner light, wisdom, mercy, and compassion you bring to this gathering. When you have offered your prayer, be seated again and breathe deeply for approximately one minute. When you are finished, say "amen" aloud and shift your attention to the sights and sounds around you. When everyone has said "amen," we will continue. *Note: Ring the bell at the end of one minute if the group has not resumed.* **(STOP)**

From the Heart journal:
A Personal Prayer Journal for Women

Turn in your journal to pages 48 and 49, "Encircled by Friends." **(STOP)** Complete as much as you can in the next five minutes. After five minutes, I will ring the bell and invite you to share what you have written. *Note: Ring the bell after five minutes.* **(STOP)**

You've Got to Have Heart

Time's up. I am moving to take the hand-sized heart from the focus center. 🛑 We will pass the heart around the circle as we share. When the heart comes to you, it is your turn to share one name and the words you chose to describe this woman. When you are finished, pass the heart to the woman on your right. We will continue in this manner until everyone has had the opportunity to share. If anyone does not wish to share, she simply passes the heart. When we are finished, we will return the heart to the focus center. Since I am holding the heart, I will share first. _Note: After you share, pass the heart to the woman on your right. When all others in the circle who wish to share have done so and the heart has made its way back to you, return it to the focus center._ 🛑 ♥

A Heart-Centered Story

The Quest of the Woman in Search of Her Heart

Chapter 5

In Chapter 4, we heard Sage tell Questa that there is no map to guide her to her heart. "You find your heart when you open yourself to receive it," Sage told her. Then Sage told Questa a story about a woman who was offered living water and another story about Mary, who had faith in God's divine will for her life. As the chapter closed, Questa was beginning to seek God's will for her life. She learned that finding her true heart begins with accepting who she is. As you continue the story, remember to read slowly and thoughtfully.

Sage and the woman without a heart continue their walk. They come to a spring and sit down on the rocks that surround it. They sit in silence. After removing their shoes, they place their feet into the small pool. ♥

"Do you feel the wonderful coolness of the spring?" Sage asks. Questa is beginning to understand that seemingly simple questions usually hold deeper lessons.

"Yes," Questa answers. She waits.

Sage moves closer. She looks directly at Questa. Questa feels the nearness of what she suspects is amazing grace. Acceptance. Tenderheartedness. "You don't have much compassion for yourself, do you?" asks Sage.

"Maybe not. Not anymore," says Questa.

"It's an illusion to think we have compassion for others when we don't have it for ourselves," says Sage, as if reading Questa's mind. "We cannot care for others when we have little, if any, forgiveness for our own humanness." ♥

"That may be the rule for most people, but it is not true with me. I am forgiving toward others. I'm only hard on myself. My mother was always telling me, 'You can do and be anything you want.' To me, she was saying, 'You have to try harder. You have to be perfect.' "

"And do you follow that advice?" asks Sage.

"Sure. And it worked at first," says Questa. "At least I think it did. I was considered successful. Now I'm tired. I feel I've lost something somewhere along the way." ♥

"And has trying harder at what you've been doing made you more of the person you want to be?" Sage asks. Another long wait. Then Sage answers her own question. "My guess is that you are more the person you long to be as you sit here by this spring."

"Here I am more myself. I feel free here," says Questa sadly. ♥

After a long pause, Sage says, "It's hard to forgive life for not giving you what you want. It's even harder to forgive your childhood years for the love you needed but never got. Life's not easy, and no one ever has enough in her storehouse of love from the early years to weather all the storms that come." ♥

Feelings well up inside Questa. She sighs heavily. Her voice breaks as she says, "I think I know what I've lost along the way. For one thing, I've lost faith that my life will ever be any different than it is right now." ♥

Sage shakes her head knowingly and responds, "You've lost heart—your heart. Have you also given up the idea that God can make a difference?"

With a deep sigh of resignation, Questa says, "Perhaps I have." ♥
Sage tells a story:

> There once was a woman who was bent over. For eighteen
> years she was so physically bent over that she could not
> stand up straight. One day Jesus, the healer, saw her. He said
> simply, "Woman, you are free." And she was.
>
> *(Luke 13:10-13, author's paraphrase)*

Questa and Sage again sit in silence. They have traveled far enough together to sit quietly in the hard places.

"I've been 'bent over' for a long time now," Questa says. "I am trying so hard to save myself, to be perfect, that I don't have time to really live. I don't want to live like this anymore. I want to be free." ♥

"Today you see me stand tall," says Sage. She stands as if presenting herself for inspection. "But once I, too, was fully bent over. If you want to be free, then you must become aware. When you are fully aware, life's lessons become your teacher. They can help you find your heart."

"How?" Questa asks, puzzled. She stands to face her mentor.

"Life's wisdom, God's wisdom, is all around you in your lostness. God's call to you is to stop trying to save yourself," explains Sage.

"Wait a minute," says Questa, feeling overwhelmed and a bit confused with the new direction of the conversation. She removes her feet from the water, drawing her knees to her chest. "I've been to hundreds of church services, dozens of 'how to' workshops, mission weekends, and a few women's retreats. They give me a time out. I come away feeling good. But nothing permanent happens inside. Life goes on pretty much as it has." ♥

"Did any of them talk about heart and Spirit?" Sage inquires.

"Sure. Maybe. A bit," responds Questa. "Mostly we sat and listened to motivational speakers get up and tell us things about God and the Bible. Once in a while a social or moral issue was thrown in. Some talked about how to raise the kids or enhance a marriage." ♥

Sage says, "Perhaps you are looking in the wrong places to find your heart. The heart's deepest lessons are often where you least expect to find them. And sometimes the ways are hard. I know a woman who attends church every week. One day she discovered a new teacher: abortion. ♥

"This woman's daughter decided to have an abortion; and after much thought and many tears, the woman decided to support her. Afterward, a chasm grew between them. Each pretended to the other that nothing had happened. Like many of us, they didn't talk about it. The woman felt unable to go to her church friends, fearful of their judgment. Finally, she sought out a Christian woman for counsel. ♥

"In tears the mother spilled out her story to the counselor. She told how she had felt a deep sense of aloneness and disappointment. She talked about her anger at the lack of help and support that she and her daughter had received. ♥

"She explained to the counselor that she once had told a friend about her daughter's abortion. Her well-meaning friend had said that her feelings of guilt pointed to a bad decision. That had only added to her sense of worthlessness and loss of hope. ♥

"The mother finished relating her anguished story. Only then did her counselor respond. She spoke a word of compassion and grace. The counselor said: 'Abortion was something you'd hoped that you would never need to face. But you did. You supported your daughter's choice to end her pregnancy—an extremely difficult decision. It was not made lightly but with much thought and many tears. And now you are both continuing to agonize over that decision, trying to understand it. You are sad that you felt unable to turn to your faith community. You were afraid that friends would not understand the complexities of your life. It is natural to feel disappointment toward those who, for whatever reason, were not sensitive to your loss, fear, and confusion. ♥

" 'Be gentle with yourself,' the counselor continued. 'Healing takes time. Facing the hurt is a first step.' The counselor leaned forward in her chair. Taking the woman's hand, she said, 'Talking to God and being honest with God about all our doubts and fears is part of the soul-searching process that leads to healing. Go slowly so the wounds can be thoroughly cleansed. And remember that God is always gracious and loving.'

"The mother returned to her life and, in time, was able to share the counselor's words with her daughter. Together they learned to accept that they were not perfect. 'There is no room for recrimination over our lack of perfection,' the mother had said to her tearful daughter. 'We may not be perfect, but God is gracious. God is love.' " ♥

Sage and Questa sit in silence for a long time. The sounds of the spring run between them.

"That is a powerful story," Questa says softly, remembering her own unrevealed secrets. In the tenderness of the moment, she tells Sage of the deep hidden sadness she carries. Relief washes over her as she finally shares her burden with another after so many years.

Sage squeezes her hand. "In life we encounter teachers every day. Mostly we avoid them. The mother's and daughter's fears almost hid the real lesson. Often it is the very crisis we run from that brings us face to face with our heart."

Heart. Compassion. Questa ponders each word. Only a week ago the woman without a heart would not have been able to hear these words of compassion and grace. Now she begins to see compassion as the opposite of fear. ♥

"With each decision, we grow in wisdom and insight," Sage says. "We gain clarity as we make new decisions. In each new challenge we grow in grace, compassion, and knowledge. Soon you will be able to embrace your joy as easily as you take hold of your sorrow." ♥

Questa looks Sage straight in the eye for the first time and, with a strong, steady voice, says, "Perhaps it is time for me to forgive myself, to accept life's twists and turns, and to move on."

And somewhere in the distance she hears the echo of her teacher, Jesus: "Woman, you are free." To be continued. . . . ♥

Heartbeat

Note: Choose a selection from the "Meditative" category on page 201 of the "Bibliography of Suggested Music," or another song, and listen quietly as you prepare yourselves for "Sacred Story Bible Study" or for the journaling exercise on page 104

Sacred Story Bible Study

Note: If this is a thirty-minute gathering, or if your group will not be doing the Bible study together for another reason, move on to the next

section. Take some time this week to read and reflect on the Sacred Story.

In this exercise we will use again the "Opening Hearts" method of "Sacred Story Bible Study." Using this approach, we will read the text, write in our journals, and listen to one another's reflections. As a result, we will search our hearts and discern what God is saying to us. Remember, this is not a time for discussion. Instead, the study emphasizes listening and reflecting on the Scripture.

If there are more than five women in our full group, we will divide into small circles of three to five by choosing women whom we know the least. We will space our groups around the room and circle our chairs so that we are sitting knee to knee. Each group will need to choose a facilitator, who will guide her group through the entire Sacred Story exercise. We will remain in quiet reflection and prayer until all of the groups are finished. 🛑 ♥

Opening Hearts
Note: The small group facilitator begins reading here.

Turn in your journal to page 50, "Opening Hearts Sacred Story Bible Study: Freedom." 🛑 I will read the directions, pausing at each step so that we may work through the process together. 🛑

Note: Follow the directions on pages 50–53 in your journal to complete the study. When finished, return quietly to the larger circle and fast from speech until everyone has completed the study. 🛑 ♥

From the Heart Journal:
A Personal Prayer Journal for Women

In a few moments we will fast from speech for ten minutes. This means we will stop all talk from the moment we begin journaling until time is up. Now turn in your journal to pages 54 and 55, "Pieces and Puzzles of My Hard Times." 🛑

After this time apart, we will not take time in our gathering to share what we have written. If you choose, you may make an appointment with a *Heart to Heart* friend with whom you feel especially connected to discuss your written reflections at another time.

Now I invite you to find a quiet space and claim it as your own. You may move to another part of the room, another room, or even outside to write. I will let you know when time is up by ringing the bell. We then will come back to the larger group and break our silence with a closing prayer ritual. *Note: Ring the bell after ten minutes.* 🛑♥

Heartbeat

Note: Play gentle, soothing music in the background during the closing prayer ritual to cover up distracting sounds and help put everyone at ease. Choose from the "Meditative" category on page 201 in the "Bibliography of Suggested Music," or choose another song. Begin playing the music after you have discussed scheduling arrangements for the next gathering.

A Hearty Goodbye

Gathering 6 will take place on *(date/s)* at *(time/s and place/s)*. *Note: If you are using the multiple groups format, explain that participants may attend any scheduled gathering. If the group needs to discuss meeting dates, times, and places, do so now.* 🛑

Choose a small candle from the focus center. Then stand by your chair. 🛑 *Note: During the following prayer ritual, pause at least ten seconds at each* 🛑 .

The candle is yours to take home. Put it in a special place. Light it at least once a day, perhaps while you are having your morning coffee or before turning out the light at bedtime. Light it to remember "the way of compassion" toward yourself and, therefore, toward others. Pray for God's awareness of the places where you may be a compassionate, merciful presence in a difficult world. Remember yourself, your family, your community, and other *Heart to Heart* women in your group. 🛑 ♥

Notice its shape, size, and color. 🛑 Now move your gaze to the candle's flame. (STOP)   See the whites, yellows, and blues within the flame. Again move your gaze to the aura of light that extends beyond the flame. (STOP)   Watch the light flicker. (STOP)   Now close your eyes and picture your candle in your mind's eye.(STOP) See its shape, size, and color. (STOP) See in your imagination the colors of white, yellow, and blue at the wick.(STOP) Notice the aura of light that extends beyond the flame.(STOP) Watch it flicker. (STOP)   Now carry that aura from your imagination to your heart. (STOP) You may open your eyes. (STOP)

Jesus said, "You are the light of the world" (*Matthew 5:14a*). You carry this aura, this Christ-light, with you as you leave here. Stop now and take a long, deep breath.(STOP)   Hold it for a count of ten. (STOP)   Now blow it out as you extinguish your candle.(STOP)

Let's say our closing prayer together:(STOP)

I am a woman living in the light and heart of God. Amen.

Remember to take off your nametag and place it on the focus center as you leave. As I extinguish the candle, go in God's love.(STOP)

Gathering 6

Heartbeat

Note: Find a respite from our hectic world by playing soothing music as everyone gathers. See the "Bibliography of Suggested Music" in the Appendix, pages 200–03 for selections. Choose from any of the three categories: "Meditative," "Music for Movement," or "Sing-along." You also may choose other appropriate songs.

Circle of Hearts

Note: One woman begins the gathering by reading the following aloud to the group. Remember to read at an unhurried pace, allowing time for silence. For more detailed reminders on how to open and conduct a Heart to Heart gathering, refer to "Getting Started," pages 28–32.

Welcome to *Heart to Heart*. We begin our sixth gathering with our usual heart-centered ritual. If we have not already done so, let us circle our chairs around a central table—our focus center. **STOP** I will take the articles for our gathering from the supply box and arrange them on the focus center: a cloth covering, a candle and matches (or a lighter), a heart-shaped box, a hand-sized heart, nametags, a wide-edged felt-tip pen, a bell, and a bag of feathers—one for each of us. **STOP** Remember, you have the option of saying "Pass" at any time during the gathering. Now choose a nametag—not your own—and pin it on the woman it names. When everyone has done this, we will proceed. **STOP**

Heartbeat

Note: Meditative music will help put the group in the mood for the following prayer ritual. See page 201 in the "Bibliography of Suggested Music" for ample selections, or choose other songs. Play the music quietly in the background.

Heartwarmers

Prayer is Spirit speaking to spirit, Heart calling to heart. We recognize the Spirit of God in each person. I light the candle on our focus center now to reveal to us the presence of God in our lives. **STOP** Our small gathering gives us a safe space where, together, we may practice living God's loving presence in our everyday lives.

Let us pause and practice right now. Join me in saying together these words from our teacher, Jesus. Repeat each line aloud after me: **STOP**

> **"Ask, and it will be given you; STOP**
> **search, and you will find; STOP**
> **knock, and the door will be opened for you." STOP ♥**
>
> —*Matthew 7:7*

As you focus your gaze on the lighted candle in the center of our circle, remember our promise to come to these gatherings. We gather not to make a safe, exclusive place for ourselves but to create a community of women who may begin to picture a different way of living. We are not together because we see everything the same way. Nor are we always comfortable. We are together because this is where God calls us to be—in community. The mystery of God's community is that God includes all people, no matter what our differences may be. God invites us to be sisters to one another.

Now, place your feet flat on the floor. (STOP) Join hands around the circle. (STOP) Close your eyes. (STOP) Calm your heart, and take three deep breaths as you sit in God's presence with friends. When you have finished, open your eyes. (STOP) ♥

Today there are feathers on the focus center—one for each of us. Take a feather and hold it in your hand. (STOP) We will learn the meaning of this feather in today's continuing story. For now, live fully in this present moment. Look around the room and look into your sisters' eyes. Think about each woman present. How do they bless you? What are they teaching you? For the next minute, sit in silence and think about these persons. *Note: Continue reading after one minute.* (STOP)

Let us pause again for one minute to thank God for this circle of women. Offer up a silent prayer of thanksgiving. When you finish, place your feather in front of you on the focus center as a show of thanksgiving for this community of women that breaks through the walls of fear to reveal God in our midst. When all the feathers are placed on the table, we will be ready to move on. (STOP) ♥

Now repeat aloud after me each line of the following prayer, called "The Blessing Place." (STOP)

> **Strong sisters who have walked with me,** (STOP)
> **and wept and laughed and soared with me,** (STOP)
> **Can we not yet on this life's plane** (STOP)
> **reach out, and up and up again** (STOP)
> **until by reaching, soaring, searching** (STOP)
> **at last we find the prize of living life** (STOP)
> **through women's eyes?** (STOP)
> **And then by Love and Faith and Grace** (STOP)
> **we'll share with other waiting hearts,** (STOP)
> **the treasures of this Women's Place.*** (STOP) ♥
>
> —*Deborah B. Sims*

*From *Women Psalms*, compiled by Julia Ahlers, Rosemary Broughton, Carol Koch; Saint Mary's Press, Christian Brothers Publications, Winona, Minnesota; 1992

Heartbeat

Note: Invite everyone to dance or move to a selection from the "Music for Movement" category found on pages 201–02 in the "Bibliography of Suggested Music," or choose another appropriate song. Don't be embarrassed! Get in touch with the wonderful body that God created!

A Heart-Centered Story

The Quest of the Woman in Search of Her Heart

Chapter 6

As she continued the search for her heart, Questa discovered that trying harder has not gotten her where she wants to go. Sage shared a poignant story of a woman who lived with a hard spiritual decision— not unlike many hard decisions Questa has faced. As the last chapter ended, Questa realized that crisis brings one face to face with one's heart. As you continue the story, remember to read *slowly* and thoughtfully.

Questa decides to walk farther after Sage leaves her to return to the house. Dusk begins to descend, and Questa loses her way. She skids forward on a bushy slope and falls on her backside, skinning her leg. While she is down, she takes the opportunity to survey her surroundings, searching for clues where to go next. First, she finds the big oak, then the little stream, and finally the bridge that leads to the house. Questa arrives back at the door in the last twilight. ♥

"I was about to send a search party out to look for you," Sage says as she stands at the kitchen counter, smiling. Is she amused or relieved? It crosses Questa's mind to be wary of Sage. Sage knows too much about her to be trusted. Questa has a history of loving people until they get too close. But all of those relationships took care of themselves when Questa moved on. ♥

Sage notices the dried blood on Questa's leg. "What happened?" she asks with concern.

"A close encounter of the embarrassing kind," Questa replies, looking down at her feet.

"Here. Let me clean it off," offers Sage.

"It's OK. I'll be fine," Questa says, indignantly, brushing aside Sage's offer.

"Sit down." Sage speaks sternly. "I'll be right back." ♥

Questa protests weakly while Sage washes the cut. Her touch is gentle. She applies ointment and a bandage. Her care feels genuine. "It's hard for you to ask for or receive help, isn't it?" Sage says. It is more a statement than a question. Questa looks away. ♥

"After you started back to the house," Questa says, steering the conversation in a different direction, "I remembered a mealtime prayer from when I was a child." ♥

Sage remains quiet. Questa shares the prayer: "God is great; God is good. Now we thank him for our food. By God's hand we all are fed. Give us, Lord, our daily bread." ♥

"Do you still pray?" Sage inquires.

When had Questa thought about prayer before today? She searches her memory. "Occasionally at mealtimes and at church," she responds.

"Only occasionally?" asks Sage.

"I used to pray, to talk things over with God. Then, gradually, I stopped. It seemed so perfunctory. I guess I stopped believing it really makes any difference," Questa says with a sigh of resignation. ♥

Sage makes a pot of coffee. As she places the cups on a tray, Sage leads the way to a bench beside a small trickling garden pool behind the house. Water lilies are blooming there. Sage lights the lantern overhead. They sip the warm coffee in the relaxing glow of the full moon. Sage tosses bread to the fish. After a spell of quiet, Sage rises from the bench and kneels, retrieving a colorful feather floating on the water. She hands it to the woman without a heart. ♥

"I feel sad for you," says Sage. "Prayer is God's intimate conversation with your heart. Prayer is your heart-song—God's heart-song to you."

"My heart-song?" Questa repeats, listening with a new ear.

"God's Spirit within, touching your heart, knows things that your intellect does not," Sage explains. "Your heart-song—what connects you to God, and God to you—sustains you through the trials of the journey. Prayer is God's care for you." ♥

After a brief silence, Sage continues: "You fear change. Yet you have survived many changes already. The fact that you are here says that your life even now has taken an unexpected turn. No matter what goodness or evil, exhilaration or heartache comes your way, you will discover that there is always another side to you where you can go—a place that is good and fine. Your heart-song is always waiting for you. ♥

"That place is free but costly to find. Yet once you find it, once you 'get there,' you discover you can recover from grief, loss, and pain. You learn that you can be put back together without needing to understand how or why. You stop anesthetizing yourself to lessen the pain. You can simply be still and accept the truth that you are absolutely new. You will never go back to your old self again. You will never again get so lost that you cannot get back. You will not let clutter pile up or dust settle over your heart. No matter what happens, you will not misplace your heart again.

"When you keep in touch with your heart-song, you remember that God's Spirit always will carry you through." ♥

Questa feels Sage's hand rest upon her arm. Her touch is compassionate and nonjudgmental. Sage's gentle spirit helps Questa find the faith to lean into her painful memories—broken relationships, unexpected losses, abandonment, disappointments, a friend's betrayal, grief for what would never be, slights and mistakes. Questa's old ghosts rush forward. ♥

"Tragedy and disappointment enter every life," Sage says. "Each person has at least one story to tell that would break your heart."

Sage touches the feather now cradled in Questa's hand. "Let me read to you from the ancient text," Sage says as she reaches into her pocket and pulls out what appears to be a book of verse. She turns to Psalm 139. ♥

O LORD, you have searched me and known me.
        You know when I sit down and when I rise up;

Where can I go from your spirit?
        Or where can I flee from your presence?
If I take the wings of the morning

and settle at the farthest limits of the sea,
even there your hand shall lead me,
and your right hand shall hold me fast. ♥
—*Psalm 139:1, 2a, 7, 9-10*

Sage leans over on the bench and, holding out her arms, gathers Questa in. In that moment, the world itself wraps around the woman who has lost her heart and holds her tight. Questa knows that her friend's smile and touch will be hers the rest of her days. ♥

Sage places the book in Questa's hands, saying it is a gift. Then she softly leaves the garden. Questa, the woman with the hole where her heart used to be, sits quietly for a long spell—sometimes reading; more often staring off into the quiet of her heart-song. ♥

Then, in her need to feel closeness, she places the feather in that soft place between her breasts. In that moment her chest begins to feel lighter than it has for years. She takes a deep, deep breath as a refreshing breeze sweeps over her. Closing her eyes, she takes a second breath. As she exhales a third deep breath, she senses a fluttering in her chest. She has been waiting to exhale for so long. Can her heart once again take flight? Can she learn to fly on the wings of the dawn? Could it be that she is on the verge of finding her first true heart-song? *To be continued. . . .* ♥

From the Heart Journal:
A Personal Prayer Journal for Women

Take your feather from the focus center and cradle it in your hand. **STOP** Now we will take a time of solitude, a time apart to search our own hearts. Turn in your journal to page 57, "The Wings of the Morning." **STOP** I will read the directions aloud. **STOP**

During the next ten minutes we will fast from speech. This means we stop all talk from the moment we begin journaling until time is up. Find a quiet space to claim as your own. You may move to another part of the room, another room, or outside to write. I will let you know when time is up. We will not share after this journaling exercise but will move on to the next activity. *Note: Ring the bell after ten minutes to draw the circle back together.* **STOP**

Sacred Story Bible Study

Note: If this is a thirty-minute gathering, or if your group will not be doing the Bible study together for another reason, move on to the next section. Take some time this week to read and reflect on the Sacred Story.

Today we will be using the "Imagine This!" method of "Sacred Story Bible Study," which we first used in our second gathering. As you recall, the Sacred Story is read aloud three times. After each reading, you will be instructed to close your eyes and use your imagination to discover the story's meaning to you.

If there are more than five women in our full group, we will divide into small circles of three to five by choosing women whom we know the least. We will space our groups around the room and circle our chairs so that we are sitting knee to knee. Each group will need to choose a facilitator, who will guide her group through the entire Sacred Story exercise. We will remain in quiet reflection and prayer until all of the groups are finished. **STOP** ♥

Imagine This!

Note: The small group facilitator begins reading here.

Turn in your journal to page 58, "Imagine This! Sacred Story Bible Study: The Touch." **STOP** I will read each step, pausing as indicated so that we may follow the instructions and reflect on the Scripture. **STOP**

Note: Follow the directions on pages 58–59 in your journal to complete the study. When finished, return quietly to the larger circle and fast from speech until everyone has completed the study. When all have finished, proceed with the closing prayer ritual. **STOP** ♥

A Hearty Goodbye

Gathering 7 will take place on *(date/s)* at *(time/s)*. *Note: If you are using the multiple groups format, explain that participants may attend any scheduled gathering. If the group needs to discuss meeting dates, times, and places, do so now.* **STOP**

Notes: The person facilitating the following prayer ritual may not be able to participate fully. Pause at least ten seconds at each **STOP**.

Now sit quietly and place both feet on the floor. **STOP** Set aside anything that is in your hands or lap.🛑 Close your eyes, or focus on the candle's light. 🛑 Take a long, deep breath. 🛑 Hold it for a count of ten. 🛑 Now blow it out. 🛑 When everyone has opened her eyes, we will stand. 🛑

Earlier in our gathering, each of us received a feather. Cradle your feather in your hands now for a few moments. 🛑 Now give your feather to the woman on your right as you receive the feather from the woman on your left. You will take this feather home with you. *Note: Allow time for everyone to pass her feather; then continue.* 🛑

Sage tells Questa that the search for her heart requires spiritual work, both internal and external. She needs to search out her own soul. She is to pay attention to her fear but not let it rule her life.

Place the feather near your bed, perhaps with a candle, or put it in another special place—somewhere you will see it each day until we gather again. You may carry it close to your bosom, if you choose. Let it remind you that outward problems are only symptoms of something much deeper; that our hearts seek relationships rooted in community; that our hearts seek God. ♥

The woman who lives with a hole where her heart used to be is also searching to find her heart in community. She must find faith to ask for what she needs. As she begins to listen to God's song—her heart-song—she embarks on a mysterious odyssey, one that depends on faith that God's will is being worked in her life. ♥

Let us quiet ourselves as we prepare to close. Focus on the candle's light or close your eyes as you hear these words of Jesus: "Daughter, your faith has made you well; go in peace" (*Luke 8:48*).

Let's say our closing prayer together. Repeat after me: 🛑

I am a woman living in the heart of God. Amen. 🛑 ♥

As we close, plant your feet on the floor and free your hands of all objects. 🛑 With eyes still closed, take a deep breath in. 🛑 Hold it. 🛑 Now blow it out. 🛑

Remember to take off your nametag and place it on the focus center as you leave. As I extinguish the candle, go in God's love.

Gathering 7

Heartbeat

Note: Play some stirring, energizing music as everyone gathers. Raise the energy level in the room! Choose from the Music for Movement category on pages 201–03 in the "Bibliography of Suggested Music," or choose other appropriate music. Then boogie down!

Circle of Hearts

Note: One woman begins the gathering by reading the following aloud to the group. Remember to read slowly, allowing time for reflection as appropriate. For more detailed reminders on how to open and conduct a Heart to Heart gathering, refer to "Getting Started," pages 28–32.

Welcome to Gathering 7. Congratulations for making time today for your heart. If we have not already done so, let us circle our chairs around a central table—our focus center. It serves to remind us of God's presence. **STOP** Now I will take the articles for our gathering from the supply box and arrange them on the focus center: a cloth covering; a candle and matches (or a lighter); a heart-shaped box; a hand-sized heart; nametags; a wide-edged felt-tip pen; scissors; a bell; a long, knotted cord made of silken material; and large prayer beads. *Note: Be sure that the long, knotted cord is placed in a circle around* *the edge of the table. The number of prayer beads you use will depend on the size of your group. If in a large group, provide one bead for each woman. If in a small group, you may provide enough beads so that everyone may choose one bead to represent each woman in the group.* 🛑

Take a moment now to choose a nametag from the focus center and take it to a sister. Pin it on her and offer her an affirming word, a genuine compliment. When everyone has finished and returned to her seat, we will continue. 🛑 ♥

Heartbeat

Note: During "Heartwarmers," you may want to play a selection from the "Meditative" category on page 201 in the "Bibliography of Suggested Music," or play another song of your choice.

Heartwarmers

I light the candle on our focus center to remind us of God's listening presence. 🛑

Repeat after me these words of our teacher, Jesus: 🛑

"Blessed are the pure in heart, 🛑
for they will see God." 🛑
—Matthew 5:8

Where your treasure is there will your heart be also.

The process of awakening to a pure heart is slow. It takes "holy listening." Awakening comes as we open ourselves to hear wisdom speak. Day by day, we learn how to be more attentive listeners. Intentionally spending time in prayerful listening facilitates our relationships with others, ourselves, and God. The greatest gift we can give is to let go of our own preoccupations so that we can hear one another. This is a blessing both to one another and to us.

I invite each woman to come and select a bead—or beads—from the focus center. *Note: If in a large group, each woman chooses one bead. If in a small group and enough beads have been purchased, participants may choose one bead to represent each woman present.* (STOP) Christians in the tenth century used a string of knots to pray the Lord's Prayer and other repetitive prayers. Such prayer became common in every part of Europe, aided by prayer beads—pebbles, berries, or threaded disks of bone. Prayer beads are also common to other ancient religions such as Buddhism and Islam. Their use can be traced as far back as ancient Nineveh. Like the ancient prayer beads, the beads we hold in our hands today will assist us in our prayer. ♥

As we enter into a time of relaxation and silent prayer, let us draw together with truly listening hearts. Eastern Orthodox writers advise us to let our minds descend into our hearts. As we descend, we enter into communion with one another and with God.

Note: The person facilitating the following prayer ritual may not be able to participate fully. Pause at least ten seconds at each (STOP).

Sit calmly with a pure heart. Ready yourself to listen to your heart's awakening. Close your eyes. (STOP) Free your hands and lap of all objects. (STOP) Put one hand on your stomach and the other on your chest. (STOP) Inhale slowly, so that your stomach expands.(STOP) Exhale slowly, so that your stomach contracts. (STOP) Imagine that your belly button is touching your spine. Deep, slow breathing helps you calm down and focus on this time with God. Take three deep breaths, pausing between each breath. As you breathe, listen for God. When you are finished, open your eyes. (STOP)

You've Got to Have Heart

Taking your prayer bead with you, pair off with someone you do not know well. Move your chairs so that you are facing each other. Pause together for one minute of silence before you begin sharing. You are responsible for keeping your own time. Then ask each other, **"Since we last met, when did you feel your heart 'awakening'?"**

Take turns answering the question. Each of you has two minutes to talk. Again, you are responsible for keeping your own time. When you finish, sit together in silence. When the room is quiet, I will give further instructions. Remember: one minute of silence, two minutes for the first person to talk, two minutes for the second person to talk, and then silence. Let's begin. *Note: When all are finished and the room is silent, continue.* 🛑

Now, exchange beads and spend one more minute in prayer for your partner. Hold hands if you wish. Close your eyes and picture your prayer partner's face. Silently lift up a prayer of thanksgiving. I will let you know when the minute is up. Begin now. *Note: Ring the bell after one minute.* 🛑

When you are ready, return the bead to your partner and give her some sign of appreciation and care—a hug, a handshake, or a kind word. Then rejoin the larger circle. 🛑 ♥

A Heart-Centered Story

The Quest of the Woman in Search of Her Heart

Chapter 7

In our last episode, Questa returned from a hike wounded. Sage cared for her friend's hurts—of both body and heart. Sage soothingly read an ancient heart-song that summoned spirit and care from the Psalms. Questa was beginning to take to heart the ancient lessons.

There is truth beyond rationality. Can Questa find her own wings? Will her spirit ever fly again? She is on the verge of finding her first, true heart-song. As you continue the story, remember to read slowly and thoughtfully.

———————

Questa takes her cup of coffee out on the porch and surveys the darkening sky. It's her favorite time of day, when all thoughts of what must get done stop. She draws her sweater tightly around her, staving off the cold. Where has summer gone? The weather takes a surprising turn, and a light snow begins to blanket the trees and grass. She likes it. The whiteness softens things. ♥

Questa is thinking about love. The word holds tremendous power. She loves her friends, her pets, her far-flung family. She loves the church—but only in a general way, not as specific individuals. She hardly knows them. ♥

People talk about love at weddings, but who talks openly about love at other times? Whom does she love? Who loves her? Her parents' confusing statement to her about love was the standard: "I may not always like the things you do, but I will always love you." What did that mean? ♥

Questa knows some people love her because she sees and does things their way. They like her when she is being who they want her to be. But who loves and treasures her as she is? She writes the question in her journal in order not to forget it. ♥

Questa climbs into her car and drives the short distance to the "mom and pop" grocery store in town. The ride is uneventful. On the trip back, however, the snowfall turns heavy and wet. She pulls onto the shoulder of the road and turns off the engine. Silence. She loves moments like this. Solitude. She has time to think—and even pray. She is moving more and more toward her heart-song. ♥

At Sage's suggestion, Questa has started to keep a journal. In it she writes little that has meaning to others. What does it matter? It is only for her—nothing formal. The book is a place to record thoughts, moments, patterns, dreams, and insights that spring up in unexpected moments and leave just as quickly. Like little elves, elusive, she catches them before they vanish. ♥

Questa climbs out of the car and surveys the snow-covered landscape around her. The flakes, tumbling one upon the other, land on her upward-turned face. Maybe she will stay here. She is tempted to lie down on this soft carpet of white . . . close her eyes . . . go to sleep. In the past, moments like this would have bred irritation. Tonight, the still moment speaks to her of love. She has grown to love Sage. Yet she feels a restlessness within, a need to move on, to go back to her life. Will Sage understand? ♥

Questa hears a truck—moving closer, droning. The truck throws cinders on the road, and Questa gets back into her car to follow behind. It is almost midnight when she arrives back at the house. A light glows from the kitchen. Sage is waiting for her as Questa had hoped she would be. ♥

"You must be exhausted," Sage says, as Questa stomps snow from her boots and shakes off her coat on the entrance rug.

"You didn't need to wait up," says Questa. She spots the cup of coffee on the counter, waiting for her.

"Why not?" asks Sage. "You would have done the same for me." ♥

They settle on the counter stools. "I pulled over, " Questa tells her. "I couldn't see three feet in front of me."

"What did you do then?" asks Sage.

"I got out of the car and watched the snow," Questa says. "And I thought about love—what I give and what I receive, and if it is enough." She pauses, then continues: "You've given me love since the first time I walked in here. I didn't understand love. I thought it was sexual, or something you feel for children or kittens. I thought people gave love in hopes of a big return. All I knew was that it didn't seem to work for me." ♥

Both women were growing sleepy. "Perhaps we can pick up this conversation in the morning before you leave, when we are fresh," says Sage.

"How did you know I need to leave?" asks Questa. ♥

"I sensed it," responds Sage. "It's time for you to move back into your world. That is the next step of your journey. If you truly want to know yourself, then you must live side-by-side with those whose opinions, needs, and lifestyles clash with your own. If you remain here and shelter yourself from the give-and-take of relationships, you can maintain the illusion of how 'nice' you are. But as you dare to move out into the world, you will confront in yourself what you must overcome in order to take the next step toward finding your heart. You're awake now. And you are asking the hard questions." Sage stands up and turns toward the stairs. "We'll talk in the morning after you pack."

Questa nods. She reaches out clumsily to give Sage a quick hug, but she can't seem to let go. Questa stays in the embrace and begins to cry. It has been a long day. She cries until she can't cry anymore; then she climbs the steps to bed. *To be continued . . .* ♥

Sacred Story Bible Study

Note: If this is a thirty-minute gathering, or if your group will not be doing the Bible study together for another reason, move on to the next

section. Take some time this week to read and reflect on the Sacred Story.

Being attentive to God means spending time with the Sacred Stories. When we listen carefully with our hearts as well as our heads, God's Word touches us in greater ways than we ever imagined possible. Today we will again use the Sacred Story Bible Study method Praying the Scripture.

If there are more than five women in our full group, we will divide into small circles of three to five by choosing women whom we know the least. We will space our groups around the room and circle our chairs so that we are sitting knee to knee. Each group will need to choose a facilitator, who will guide her group through the entire Sacred Story exercise. We will remain in quiet reflection and prayer until all of the groups are finished. **STOP** ♥

Praying the Scripture

Note: The small group facilitator begins reading here.

Turn in your journal to page 62, "Praying the Scripture Sacred Story Bible Study: Keep Awake."**STOP** I will read the directions, pausing at each step so that we may work through the process together. **STOP**

Note: Follow the directions on pages 62–65 in your journal to complete the study. When finished, return quietly to the larger circle and fast from speech until everyone has completed the study. **STOP**♥

From the Heart Journal:
A Personal Prayer Journal for Women

Turn in your journal to page 66, "A Letter to God." **STOP** During the next ten minutes, we will take time apart and fast from speech while

we reflect and write a letter to God in our journals. Our letters will remain private; we will not share what we have written after we regroup. I will let you know when time is up. **STOP** *Note: Ring the bell after ten minutes.* **STOP** ♥

Heartbeat

Note: Join in singing a "Sing-along" song from the selections listed on pages 202–03 in the "Bibliography of Suggested Music," or choose another appropriate song. Then play a "Meditative" selection to slow the pace for the closing prayer ritual. See page 201 in the "Bibliography of Suggested Music," or pick another song of your choice. Continue playing meditative music until the end of the gathering.

A Hearty Goodbye

God calls not the hardhearted, but the tenderhearted. God calls not those who have all the answers, but those who are willing to live with the questions. In living with the questions, someday we will gradually—bit by bit, step by step, without even noticing—live our way into the answer. ♥

Stand with me. **STOP** I am taking the silken cord and scissors from the focus center. **STOP** Now let us lightly weave the cord between our fingers. **STOP** This cord reminds us of our sacred connection to one another, to all women, to all the earth; we are woven together in God's love. Let us pause to visualize these connections. **STOP** Now, one at a time, each of us will cut a length of cord by cutting above the knot closest to the end; we will keep this piece as a reminder of our connections. *Note: Allow time for everyone to complete the task; then continue.* **STOP**

Now, thread your prayer bead(s) onto the piece of cord you have cut, inserting the cord through the hole in the bead(s). Then tie the ends of the cord together. *Note: Allow time for everyone to complete the task; then continue.* **STOP** ♥

Gathering 8 will take place on *(date/s)* at *(time/s and place/s)*. *Note: If you are using the multiple groups format, explain that participants may attend any scheduled gathering. If the group needs to discuss meeting dates, times, and places, do so now.* **STOP**

We will close our gathering with individual prayers for each woman standing in this circle. One at a time, each of us will pass our bead necklaces around the circle, beginning with the woman to our right. As each of us receives a bead necklace, we will hold it in our palm and offer a silent prayer for the special woman to whom it belongs. When the woman sitting to the left of the bead necklace's owner receives it, she will stand and place it around the owner's neck. I will begin. When my bead necklace is placed around my neck, the woman on my right will pass her bead necklace. We will continue in this manner until everyone has been prayed for. Does everyone understand the process? *Note: Pause for any questions, allowing anyone in the group to answer; then begin.* (STOP)

Now pray with me this ecumenical text of the Lord's Prayer. Let us pray in the softness of a whisper. (STOP)

> **Our Father in heaven,**
> **hallowed be your name,**
> **your kingdom come,**
> **your will be done, on earth as in heaven.**
> **Give us today our daily bread.**
> **Forgive us our sins**
> **as we forgive those who sin against us.**
> **Save us from the time of trial**
> **and deliver us from evil.**
> **For the kingdom, the power, and the glory are yours**
> **now and for ever. Amen.*** ♥

Note: The person facilitating may not be able to participate fully in the following relaxation exercise. Pause at least ten seconds at each (STOP) *.*

Now put everything out of your hands and lap so that you may relax. (STOP) Place your feet flat on the floor. (STOP) Close your eyes. (STOP) Take a deep breath. (STOP) Hold it for a count of ten. (STOP) Blow it out. (STOP) Now open your eyes. (STOP)

Remember to place your nametag on the focus center as you leave. (STOP) As I extinguish the candle, say to the sister sitting on either side of you, "Go in God's peace." (STOP)

*From *The United Methodist Hymnal,* 894; copyright 1989, The United Methodist Publishing House, Nashville, Tennessee.

Gathering 8

Heartbeat

Note: Play "fun" music as you gather. Choose from the "Music for Movement" or "Sing-along" categories, found on pages 201–03 in the "Bibliography of Suggested Music," or play other appropriate songs.

Circle of Hearts

Note: One woman begins the gathering by reading aloud to the group. Read slowly and thoughtfully, allowing time for reflection as appropriate. For more detailed reminders on how to open and conduct a Heart to Heart gathering, refer to "Getting Started," pages 28–32.

Welcome! It is good to be taking this time to challenge ourselves and to discover how to be faithful amid the many changes of our lives. If we have not already done so, let us circle our chairs around a central table—our focus center. **STOP** Now I will take the articles for our gathering from the supply box and arrange them on the focus center: a cloth covering, a candle and matches (or a lighter), a heart-shaped box, a hand-sized heart, nametags, a wide-edged felt-tip pen, a bell, a bag containing stick-on labels with names written on them, envelope #1, and baggies filled with confetti glitter or paper glitter. **STOP**

Now, search out the woman whose birthday is closest to your own. You may find that you share a birthday with someone here. After you locate each other, go together to the focus center, pick up your nametags, and pin them on each other. Then express a genuine thanks-

125

giving to each other and return to your seats. When everyone is finished, we will continue. 🛑 ♥

Heartbeat

*Note: Choose a song from the "Sing-along" selections listed on pages
202–03 in the "Bibliography of Suggested Music," or choose another
appropriate song. Sing along as you feel comfortable. Don't be shy!*

Heartwarmers

I light the candle on our focus center to remind us of God's faithful presence to us, as well as to remind us to be present to one another. 🛑 Listen
to these words of our teacher, Jesus. Repeat them after me: 🛑

"You shall love the Lord your God with all your heart, 🛑
     and with all your soul, 🛑
     and with all your mind." 🛑
     This is the greatest and first commandment. 🛑
     And a second is like it: 🛑
     "You shall love your neighbor as yourself." 🛑 ♥
                                        —Matthew 22:37b-39

*Note: The person facilitating the following relaxation exercise may
not be able to participate fully. Remember to read slowly and deliber-
ately, pausing at least ten seconds at each* 🛑.

Sit calmly. 🛑 Close your eyes. 🛑 By remaining in the present
moment, the now, you can silence the voices clamoring for attention in
your head. Put your books down. 🛑 Open your hands on your lap.
🛑Rest your feet flat on the floor. 🛑 Relax your neck muscles by bending your head first to the left and then to the right. 🛑 Press your shoulders down and hold for a count of five. 🛑 Now release. 🛑 Do this
a second time. 🛑 Take one deep, powerful breath—deep enough to push
your belly out. Pull the air into your lungs. Feel it run down your legs
and into your feet. 🛑 Now exhale by slowly pushing the air out through
your nose. 🛑 Take two more deep breaths🛑 Now open your eyes.
🛑

The first lines of the "Serenity Prayer" are familiar. The last lines, seldom heard, may surprise you. Let us pray the entire Serenity Prayer aloud together: **(STOP)**

God, grant me the serenity
to accept the things I cannot change,
the courage to change the things I can,
and the wisdom to know the difference.
Grant me patience with the things that take time,
tolerance of the struggles of others
that may be different from my own,
appreciation for all I have,
and the willingness to get up and try again,
One day at a time. Amen. ✶♥

Heartbeat

Note: During the following body prayer, play a selection from the "Music for Movement" category found on pages 201–02 in the "Bibliography of Suggested Music," or play other appropriate music. The person facilitating may not be able to participate fully. **(STOP)**

Now we will combine music, movement, and prayer in a deliberate way. I invite everyone to stand in a comfortable position, with your feet slightly apart. **(STOP)** Breathe deeply. **(STOP)** Shake your arms. Let the energy flow down your arms and into your fingers. **(STOP)** Wiggle your fingers. **(STOP)** Continue to breathe deeply as you flex and bend your knees, **(STOP)** your shoulders, **(STOP)** and your arms. **(STOP)** Stretch and move to loosen up your joints and ease any tightness. **(STOP)**

Now close your eyes and let your face muscles relax. **(STOP)** Be aware of your body. Feel your own energy. Be awake to what your body tells you. **(STOP)**

*"The Serenity Prayer," from *Amen: Prayers and Blessings from Around the World,* compiled by Suzanne Slesin and Emily Gwathmey. Copyright 1995 by Viking Studio Books.

Ask yourself, "What is best in my life right now?" Take a deep breath and allow yourself to feel pleasure as you dwell on this "best thing." **(STOP)**

Ask yourself, "What is most enjoyable about being who I am at this season in my life?" Take a deep breath and let yourself smile as you live in this present moment. **(STOP)**

Now offer a brief prayer of thanksgiving as you continue to breathe deeply. **(STOP)**

When you are ready, slowly open your eyes. **(STOP)**

Continue to breathe deeply as you move around the room. Walk softly, swinging your arms. **(STOP)** Now flex your limbs and muscles. **(STOP)** Be aware of your body for the remainder of the music. At the end of the song, return to your seat and we will continue. **(STOP)** ♥

From the Heart Journal:
A Personal Prayer Journal for Women

There are instances in the Sacred Stories when a person takes on a new name. In this way, the person acknowledges how his or her life has changed. Just for the fun of it, there is a new name for each of us in the bag on the focus center. *Note: Take the bag of names from the focus center now.* **(STOP)**

No peeking! Reach in and take one. *Note: Pass the bag around the circle; then continue.* **(STOP)**

Read your new name to yourself silently. **(STOP)** Now we will go around the circle and read our new names aloud. I'll go first. **(STOP)** *Note: After everyone has read her new name aloud, continue.* **(STOP)**

Now turn in your journal to pages 68–69, "New Name, New Me!" **(STOP)** Now let us peel the backs from our labels and stick our new names in the designated spot in our journals. **(STOP)** *Note: Allow time for everyone to complete the task; then continue.* **(STOP)**

Now, take the next three minutes to write your initial thoughts about your new name. I will let you know when the time is up. *Note: Ring the bell after three minutes.* **(STOP)**

You've Got to Have Heart

Time is up. I am moving to take the hand-sized heart from the focus center. (STOP) We will pass the heart around the circle as we share. When the heart comes to you, it is your turn to share a short comment about your new name. When you are finished, pass the heart to the woman on your right. We will continue in this manner until everyone has had the opportunity to share. If anyone does not wish to share, she simply passes the heart. When we are finished, we will return the heart to the focus center. Since I am holding the heart, I will share first. _Note: After you share, pass the heart to the woman on your right. When all others in the circle who wish to share have done so and the heart has made its way back to you, return it to the focus center._ (STOP) ♥

A Heart-Centered Story

The Quest of the Woman in Search of Her Heart

Chapter 8

After getting caught on the road in a snowstorm, Questa pulled the car over and took time to survey her life. The still moment spoke to her of love. A restlessness within told her that it is time to move on with her life. Later that evening, in Sage's kitchen, Questa admitted that she is ready to return to her life. She told Sage that she will be leaving in the morning. Our story continues as morning breaks. As you continue the story, remember to read slowly and _thoughtfully._

The morning sunlight sparkles on the fresh snow. Questa wakes feeling confident and warm—almost her old self. She feels cared for and caring toward others.

"I came here looking for my heart," says Questa.

"And did you find it?" asks Sage. The two women pick up Questa's suitcases. ♥

Questa is silent. She squares her shoulders and walks toward the car. Sage smiles. The two women's breath forms translucent clouds in the icy air. Questa glances up at the tree branches, now drooping under the snow's weight.

"That's how I feel when I try to love someone," Questa tells Sage, pointing at the tree branches. "Sagging under the burden." Her suitcase suddenly feels heavier.

"I feel guilty that I don't have enough to give," Questa continues as she hoists the suitcase into the trunk and slams the lid. "What is love, anyway?" she asks. "And don't tell me love means never having to say you're sorry!" She remembers the melodramatic *Love Story* and smiles in spite of herself. ♥

Sage appreciates the lightness added to these tough questions. She returns the smile and replies, "When you love someone, it means extending yourself for his or her care, comfort, and growth. It means wanting the best for that person. Realistically, you can't do that for everyone who comes in and out of your life. It's simply too big a task to get your arms around." ♥

Questa bends down to pick up some snow, to feel its sterling coldness. Then she says, "Sometimes I feel as if I've had all the human traffic I can stand. All I know is that I'm tired of feeling so guilty."

"We love in much smaller ways than the expansiveness of God's heart allows," says Sage. "If you give up your guilt, then you give up your naive innocence and admit that you cannot love from your own good will or right intentions." ♥

"Guilt? Innocence? I don't understand," says Questa.

Sage explains: "Questa, your parents wanted to love you deeply and unconditionally. But inevitably, at some point, they disappointed you. Marriages end, families fracture, friends betray. Yet failure doesn't keep us from trying to love time and time again. But to love as God loves? It is only through God's gift of love to us that you and I are able to recover from the pain and love again." ♥

Questa gives Sage a quizzical look.

Sage continues: "Our heart grows larger as we grow older. It expands and becomes large enough to take in the world. Love is surrender to the joy and hurt, hope and disappointment. Here." Sage starts to give Questa three sealed envelopes. Then she sees the snowball that has formed in Questa's hand. ♥

"What are these?" Questa asks, pitching the snowball into the air. She takes the envelopes and turns them over and over in search of a clue.

"They are pieces of my heart," Sage says. "Use them well. Open the first now, if you wish, and the other two when it is time. You'll know when it is time." Sage has that knowing look Questa has grown to trust. ♥

Questa tears open the first envelope and reads it. Sage's look tells Questa she is not to ask its meaning.

The two women hug a final time. Sage is the friend Questa has always longed for. She is a companion who listens hours on end. She does not explain away Questa's mysteries, but sits with her... and listens. She doesn't analyze or diagnose. She lets Questa know that she isn't crazy—only searching. ♥

Questa inserts the first letter into its envelope and puts it with the other two in her purse. Then she slides behind the wheel. "I will miss you," she tells Sage. But she is now eager to leave. No long goodbyes. It is time—time to find her heart. ♥

"One more thing before you go," says Sage. "As you search for your heart, remember to look to God's guidance. Some people call this guidance the Holy Spirit, God's Spirit. It is this Spirit of Guidance that will tell you what to look at in yourself. Guidance will not always give you loud, step-by-step instructions. Instead, Questa, pay attention to the small voices. Then you will be attuned to God's Guidance. You may be surprised to discover God's Spirit of Guidance in both the miracles and the ordinary places of life. They are the same thing, you know." ♥

On the drive home, Questa continues to ponder Sage's words and hatches a plan. She will go home and "act normal." She pictures herself doing so—making the bed, loading the dishwasher, taking out the garbage. That's it. She will act as if nothing at all is out of the ordinary. Surely her normal life will return. But, what is normal? ♥

To get a clearer idea, Questa begins to think of the people she knows. One of her friend's life crusades is to close toilet seat lids. Is that normal? Another, a meticulous housekeeper, fills most of her days keeping her house spotless. Still another is lost in "Betty Crocker Land." She hopes that isn't normal. One of her colleagues is obsessive-compulsive about keeping papers out of her in-box. The woman next door is always on a diet. Are they normal? ♥

Now that she thinks of it, she can't come up with any examples of "normal" that she wants to emulate. If these people are normal, then abnormal will do nicely, thank you.

Perhaps she will live life in an ordinary way and give up fantasies of how life is supposed to be. Should she put away, once and for all, her perfect vision of herself and be present in the moment?

Now she reads Sage's first letter, which contains Psalm 30; and she understands the point Sage is making: Take life lightly, and your heart will return. Questa reflects. She is driving away with more than she'd come with, and it is almost laughable how pleased she feels . . . and how blessed . . . and how rich. *To be continued* . . . . ♥

Heartbeat

Note: Choose a song from the "Sing-along" selections listed on pages 201–03 in the "Bibliography of Suggested Music," or choose another appropriate song. It is recommended that you choose something a bit outlandish. If you enjoy singing, go for it! If not, listen and enjoy the music.

Sacred Story Bible Study

Note: If this is a thirty-minute gathering, or if your group will not be doing the Bible study together for another reason, move on to the next section. Take some time this week to read and reflect on the Sacred Story.

When we read the Bible, we are reading the Word of God. When we listen carefully, the Word touches us in ways that move our hearts to live God's will. We are in rhythm with the heartbeat of God. Today we will use the Responsive Listening Sacred Story Bible Study method.

If there are more than five women in our full group, we will divide into small circles of three to five by choosing women whom we know the least. We will space our groups around the room and circle our chairs so that we are sitting knee to knee. Each group will need to choose a facilitator, who will guide her group through the entire Sacred Story exercise. We will remain in quiet reflection and prayer until all of the groups are finished. **STOP** ♥

Responsive Listening

Note: The small group facilitator begins reading here.

Turn in your journal to page 70, "Responsive Listening Sacred Story Bible Study: Get Up!" I will read the directions, pausing at each step so that we may work through the process together. 🛑

Note: Follow the directions on pages 70–72 in your journal to complete the study. When finished, return quietly to the larger circle and fast from speech until everyone has completed the study. 🛑 ♥

A Hearty Goodbye

In today's episode of our continuing story, Questa left the safe haven of Sage's home, a motherly womb, to return to her complex life. Where will life take her? What will she find? To find out Sage's message to Questa, we open envelope number one. 🛑 I will pass out copies of the letter, and we will read it together. *Note: Lead the group in reading the letter aloud, which also may be found on page 73 in* From the Heart Journal: A Personal Prayer Journal for Women. *Then the next reader continues.* 🛑 ♥

We too must move back into our lives. Sometimes we long to return to the innocence we can barely remember. But with our eyes wide open—with as much clarity as we can muster—God's love carries us into the give-and-take of our days. ♥

As we prepare to leave, say aloud with me the following prayer: 🛑

During this time together, God, I've claimed a spot of serenity.
    I've been introspective, thoughtful, silent, . . .
(Pause for a count of ten; then continue.)
        and I've even laughed a bit.
        I'm sort of pleased with myself.
But in a few moments, God,
        I'm leaving here.
        And when I step out that door,
        then I'll really need your help. Amen.

Gathering 9 will take place on *(date/s)* at *(time/s and place/s)*. *Note: If you are using the multiple groups format, explain that participants may attend any scheduled gathering. If the group needs to discuss meeting dates, times, and places, do so now.* **STOP** ♥

Note: The person facilitating the following exercise may not be able to participate fully. Pause at least ten seconds at each **STOP** .

Place your books and any objects you are holding on the floor. **STOP** Put your feet flat on the floor. **STOP** Take a deep breath. **STOP** Hold it. **STOP** Now release. **STOP** As I blow out this candle, the light of God's guiding Spirit goes with you. **STOP** ♥

Before our closing, let me remind you to take off your nametag and place it on the focus center before you leave. Now, let us continue. **STOP**

The things we loved as children are often the exact things we spurn as adults. Our teacher, Jesus, tells us, "Unless you change and become like children" **STOP** (*Matthew 18:3b*). And Peter Pan reminds us that if you think good thoughts and sprinkle pixy dust, you can fly.

On the focus center is one baggie of pixy dust for each of us. Take your pixy dust and join me in this un-serious benediction. We will read the bold print together. *Note: You may want to move outdoors for this farewell.* **STOP**

A Touch of Pixy Dust

Drop a bit of pixy dust at your feet for the unfairness in life— **STOP**
　　that carrots have zero calories and cookies have a zillion,
　　that the dress you like is always the most expensive,
　　that weight comes on just walking by the refrigerator.

Toss pixy dust over your shoulders, behind you, to forget the people— **STOP**
　　who do just enough to get by,
　　who never see humor in any situation,
　　who call you "Mom" a million times an hour,
　　who cut you off on the highway and take your parking space. **STOP**

Sprinkle pixy dust in front of you to take lightly— 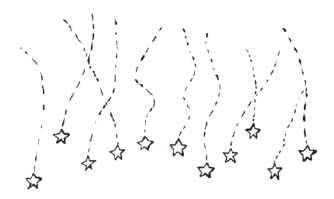 STOP
    rush-hour drivers,
    empty ice cube trays,
    long lines at the grocery store,
    and all the house and office work that's never done.

Throw pixy dust over your head to remind yourself— STOP
    that the best in life is nothing you can buy,
    that today is the day, so live it to the max,
    and that your best years in life are yet to come!

Remember to sprinkle fun through every day. As you leave, toss any remaining pixy dust on your sisters as a farewell blessing. Have fun! STOP ♥

Gathering 9

Heartbeat

Note: Play "Meditative" music as you gather; choose from the selections listed on page 201 in the "Bibliography of Suggested Music," or choose other appropriate music. Continue playing the music throughout "Circle of Hearts" and "Heartwarmers."

Circle of Hearts

Note: One woman begins the gathering by reading aloud to the group. Read at an unhurried pace. Be at home in the laughter and in the silences. For more detailed reminders on how to open and conduct a Heart to Heart gathering, refer to "Getting Started," pages 28–32.

Once upon a time, in a strange land, some women gathered on *(name the weekday)* at *(name the time of day)* to pray together, study the sacred writings, tell their stories, cry, and laugh. They touched one another's hearts and celebrated the circle that was their lives. ♥

We are those women! We gather today to continue our celebration. If we have not already done so, let us circle our chairs around a central table—our focus center. **STOP** I invite everyone to stand, move closer to the focus center, and form a circle around it. **STOP** Now I take the articles for our gathering from the supply box and arrange them on the focus center: a cloth covering, a candle and matches (or a lighter), a heart-shaped box, a hand-sized heart, nametags, a wide-edged felt-tip pen, a bell, and a ball of yarn. **STOP**

Retrieve the nametag of the person standing on your right. **STOP** As you hand it to her, briefly tell her about a kind act that someone did for you this week. When you have finished, please continue standing. We will proceed when everyone has received her nametag. (STOP) ♥

Heartwarmers

As I light the candle on the focus center, let us prepare ourselves for prayer. (STOP)

Our prayer ritual puts us in touch with a deeper reality. When rituals and ceremonies are authentic, they kindle the imagination, evoke insight, and touch the heart. Ritual weaves past, present, and future into life's ongoing tapestry. Ritual helps us face and mark the shocks, triumphs, and mysteries of everyday life. Ritual helps us experience the unseen webs of meaning, purpose, and passion that tie us together as a community of women.

May this candle represent not only God in our midst but also the Holy Spirit—who gives light, strength, and wisdom—within each woman. ♥

Let us go to our seats now and sit down. (STOP) We will take a few minutes to relax and become fully present in this circle of women.

Note: The person facilitating may not be able to participate fully in the following exercise. Pause at least ten seconds at each (STOP) .

Close your eyes and "shake off" anything that keeps you from enjoying these friends and participating with your whole self. (STOP) Free your hands of all objects. (STOP) Place your feet flat on the floor. (STOP) Take three breaths, inhaling and exhaling deeply. (STOP)

Stay a moment in the calm with your eyes closed. (STOP) Jesus shared these words of peace with his first circle of followers. Repeat each phrase after me: (STOP)

Peace I leave with you;... (STOP)
    My peace I give to you.... (STOP)
    I do not give to you as the world gives.... (STOP)
    Do not let your hearts be troubled,... (STOP)
    and do not let them be afraid.... (STOP)

—John 14:27

Now open your eyes. **(STOP)** ♥

Women have always spun fibers and woven tapestries. We connect. We create. We persevere in our labor with God to make order out of chaos, wholeness out of fragments, and beauty out of confusion. Each strand of the weave is important. The stronger threads support the weaker.

I am moving to take the ball of yarn from the focus center. **(STOP)** We will pass this ball of yarn around the circle to my right, unwinding the yarn as we pass it. As you receive the yarn, say your name. We will pause after each woman says her name so that we may lift her up in silent prayer. Then together we will say: "God bless you, (insert name)." Let us begin.**(STOP)**

Note: When you are finished, rewind the yarn and return the ball to the focus center. **(STOP)**

There are many people woven into the tapestry of your life: friends and adversaries, colleagues and competitors, family members and those whom you choose to spend time with. Think of one person—someone who is not sitting in this circle—who needs God's touch and assurance. **(STOP)** As you hold that person in your heart, lift him or her to God in prayer. Let's pause for thirty seconds of silent prayer. **(STOP)**

Note: After thirty seconds have passed, leave your seat and step into the center of the circle. Although you will not be able to participate fully in the remainder of the prayer ritual, you will be surrounded by prayer as you lead the group. **(STOP)**

Take the hands of the women sitting on each side of you. **(STOP)** Now that the circle is complete, let us pause to treasure one another and this time of prayer. Close your eyes and thank God for all that is offered—and received—here today. **(STOP)**

Pray silently for the woman on your right.**(STOP)** Pray silently for the woman on your left. **(STOP)** Now offer your heart into God's care.**(STOP)** Amen.

A Heart-Centered Story

The Quest of the Woman in Search of Her Heart

Chapter 9

In Chapter 8, Questa left the safe womb of Sage's home to return to her complex life with its strained relationships, difficult working conditions, and less-than-adequate support base. With her she took Sage's parting words of advice, which were enclosed in three envelopes. The first message read, "O LORD my God, I cried to you for help, and you have healed me. . . . You have turned my mourning into dancing; you have taken off my sackcloth and clothed me with joy, so that my soul may praise you and not be silent. O LORD my God, I will give thanks to you forever" (*Psalm 30:2, 11-12*). Chapter 9, today's installment, finds Questa writing a letter to Sage. As you begin Questa's letter, remember to read slowly and thoughtfully.

Dear Sage,

TGIF!!! I'd forgotten what a jungle it is out here, and then—a double whammy—I discovered that I'm not the queen. I guess you can tell already that returning to work is tougher than I expected. Boy, am I relieved not to be in charge of this mess. I'd forgotten how hard it is working with difficult people. But I am determined to care for my colleagues. I roam from desk to desk and office to office, stopping to chat, telling first one person and then another how I value them and the work they do. I ask about their lives and happiness. For the first time I really listen to their answers with my whole being. I am truly present with them in the moment. At noon I make it a point to stop my work and join a few others for lunch. It is embarrassing to say this, but although I've worked here for five years, this is the first time that I have begun to see each individual as worthy of my time and care. ♥

What happens? Those I supervise receive me politely. My colleagues take a "wait and see" attitude. They "remember me when." I can't blame them. If I were in their shoes, I'd be skeptical of my new behavior too.

Now that you've heard about the first discovery of my l-o-n-g week, here's a second. I've discovered that when other people at work tell me what a strong woman I am, that's just their way of laying more on me. From the moment I got back, I knew with utter certainty that when it rains it pours, and it must be my turn to get wet. I was reaching for my old answers to these kind of days—antacids and aspirin—when out of the blue it occurred to me to try an alternative. I sat at my desk and just started praying for the strength to handle the situation. I didn't have a plan or anything, but I just kept praying, "God, help me do this. Please, help me do this; help me do this." And before I knew it, I was handling it. I also learned an important lesson. But I'll tell you more about that later. ♥

Next, I decided to let my colleagues know, without a doubt, that I have changed—that I really care. I want to share my newly discovered gift of being nonjudgmental and truly concerned about others. So, I called a meeting. I gave a speech about care and trust and the freedom to grow to be who you are. I said to them, "You know, it seems to me that we work overtime finding fault with one another. It's the little things that divide us. There is always something wrong or someone to blame. I'm not saying we have to be best friends, but it would be nice to show each other respect. Or perhaps it's true that misery loves company." Then I asked them what would happen if everyone, myself included, made a decision not to say anything negative or disrespectful about another person for just one day. I am still shocked. It works. I am real with them, and they are coming to know I care. I think people are intuitive about what is authentic and what is phony. ♥

Sage, in the past, the pressures of immediate tasks and the bottom line often crowded out the needs of the people in my workplace. Now I realize that "getting there" is half the fun. Caring begins with knowing about others. It requires listening, understanding, and accepting people for who they are. It means acknowledging that each woman or man is a person of sacred worth. Love is a willingness to reach out and open one's heart. Accepting my vulnerability—dropping my mask—allows me to meet others heart to heart. I swear, there is a soul within this community. ♥

The hardest moment of the week came when Loretta walked up to me and made a sly, snide comment. If every person has a nemesis, she's mine. She has a way of pushing my buttons. She is like a fingernail on the blackboard. Loretta is just not lovable. I found myself responding with an off-handed remark. I didn't want to hear her—didn't want to understand that she had a valid point, no matter how unpleasantly expressed.

Then I recalled how many other times I had let her walk away with a rift between us. So, right there and then, I decided to put my pride in my pocket and mend my relationship with Loretta. I was wrong, and I apologized. There are still a lot of broken threads in our relationship. They will take time to mend. But now I have time . . . more than I ever dreamed.

Love,

Questa

PS: Sage, I almost forgot to tell you about the important lesson I alluded to earlier. I learned a two-letter word that makes life bearable—NO! *To be continued* . . .

Heartbeat

Note: If you have Colleen Fulmer's CD and/or songbook Her Wings Unfurled, play "The 'No' Song!" (See the "Bibliography of Suggested Music," page 203; sing out strongly on the refrain. It's excellent.) If not, simply read together the refrain printed here and then continue.

"The 'No' Song."
No! No! No! A thousand times I'll say no!
Read my lips; it's so clear, just open up your ears.
I'm sayin', No! No! No! No! No, no, no, no!
No, no, no, no, no! [No!] No, no, no, no!*

*Lyrics © Colleen Fulmer. Used by permission of Loretto Spirituality Network.

Sacred Story Bible Study

Note: If this is a thirty-minute gathering, or if your group will not be doing the Bible study together for another reason, move on to the next section. Take some time this week to read and reflect on the Sacred Story.

We want to be connected to the mystery of God. Our hungry hearts long for a mystical link to God, a link that is creative and life-giving. We seek encounters with God that feed the soul. Some of us do this intellectually; as we gain more knowledge, we come to know God. Others of us have a more intuitive relationship with God, taking into account our subjective experiences. ♥

God's Spirit works individually with each one of us. Your way of knowing may be different from that of the woman sitting beside you. We respect the different ways of knowing. The "head stuff" is not superior to the "heart stuff." For most of us, both the reasoning mind and the imaginative mind combine in our experience of God. ♥

No doubt some of us have had small revelatory experiences of God during our *Heart to Heart* experience. In our search for our hearts, we may have gained wisdom, solace, assurance, direction, and peace. Our experiences of God are real. We feel God's touch, hear God's voice, and sense God's presence. This allows us to be women full of God's creative, freeing Spirit.

As we read today's Sacred Story using the Opening Hearts method of study, let us listen not only with the head but also with the heart—for God speaks both in the voice of reason and in the intuitive whisper of love. ♥

In this exercise, we will read the text, write in our journals, and listen to one another's reflections. As we do this, we will search our hearts and discern what God is saying to us. Remember, this is not a time for discussion. Instead, the study emphasizes listening and reflecting on the Scripture.

If there are more than five women in our full group, we will divide into small circles of three to five by choosing women whom we know the least. We will space our groups around the room and circle our chairs so that we are sitting knee to knee. Each group will need to choose a facilitator, who will guide her group through the entire Sacred Story exercise. We will remain in quiet reflection and prayer until all of the groups are finished. **STOP** ♥

Opening Hearts

Note: The small group facilitator begins reading here.

Turn in your journal to page 74, "Opening Hearts Sacred Story Bible Study: A Kiss of Tears." 🛑 I will read the directions aloud, pausing at each step so that we may work through the process together. 🛑

Note: Follow the directions on pages 74–76 in your journal to complete the study. When finished, return quietly to the larger circle and fast from speech until everyone has completed the study. 🛑 ♥

From the Heart Journal:
A Personal Prayer Journal for Women

Jesus often used simple stories to convey deeper meaning. He knew that stories help transport people to the mystical realm of the Spirit. Without narrative as a vessel for the soul, it would be difficult for us to talk about some of the hard lessons of life. Stories—such as the one about the woman in search of her heart—teach, instruct, provide "psychic shelter," and heal wounds. The common tales we tell one another weave a strong fabric that can warm the coldest spiritual night. Stories transcend time and place. Stories act as the symbolic narrative that holds us together in community.

Now it is time to write a piece of *your* story. Turn to page 79 in your

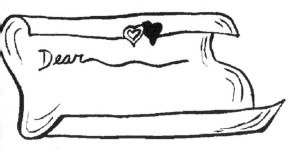

journal, "A Letter of My Heart." Follow the instructions on the journal page. During the next ten minutes, we will fast from speech and write our letters. I will let you know when time is up. When we reconvene, we will not share what we have written but will proceed with our closing prayer ritual. *Note: Ring the bell after ten minutes.* 🛑 ♥

A Hearty Goodbye

Gathering 10 will take place on *(date/s)* at *(time/s and place/s)*. *Note: If you are using the multiple groups format, explain that participants may attend any scheduled gathering. If the group needs to discuss meeting dates, times, and places, do so now.* 🛑

I am moving to the focus center to take the ball of yarn from the table. 🛑 This ball of yarn that I hold in my hands reminds us that we are linked and interwoven. Each one of us adds the strand of our life to the ever-expanding cosmic tapestry. Let us stand in a circle, away from the table, leaving an arm's distance between us. 🛑 I will hold the end of the yarn while I throw the ball to a woman across the circle. She then will hold the strand and throw the ball to someone else. We will continue until everyone is holding a strand and we all are knitted together. As you toss the ball to another, pray aloud a prayer of blessing for the woman who will catch the yarn. An example might be, "Sally, may you discover new ways of knowing God," or "Jennifer, may you enjoy days of health." I will throw the ball of yarn now. *Note: Continue in this manner until every-one is holding a strand of yarn; then proceed.* 🛑 ♥

The image of weaving helps us name our life realities. Let us careful-ly lower our newly woven tapestry and lay it on the floor. 🛑 Now let us encircle the weaving we've created and hold hands. 🛑 In just a moment we will listen to a song. As we listen, let us move in our cir-cle to the left. I will begin the song now.

Note: See "Heartbeat" for specific instructions. 🛑

Heartbeat

Note: Choose a song from the "Sing-along" category on page 00 in the "Bibliography of Suggested Music," or choose another song, and sing together. A song about weaving would be appropriate. When the song is over, continue with the following.

Repeat after me these words: 🛑

> **Spirit, on your loom we're weaving 🛑**
>   **lives entwined, a tapestry of grace. 🛑**
> **Spirit, by your love creating 🛑**
>   **'til in God, we see our sister's face.* 🛑**

We are blessed to stand in this web of support and love. As I blow out the candle, remember that you are accepted and loved. 🛑 Before you leave, turn to at least three other sisters and share a sign of appreciation. Remember to take off your nametag and place it on the focus center as you go. 🛑

---

*Adapted from the lyrics of "Weaving Wonder" by Colleen Fulmer, copyright 1989. Used by permission of Loretto Spirituality Network.

Gathering 10

Heartbeat

Note: Inspirational music builds a bridge that you can "cross over" to be fully present in your time together. Choose from the selections listed under any of the three categories in the "Bibliography of Suggested Music," pages 200–03, or choose other appropriate music.

Circle of Hearts

Note: One woman begins the gathering by reading aloud to the group. Read slowly, allowing time for reflection as appropriate. For more detailed reminders on how to open and conduct a Heart to Heart gathering, refer to "Getting Started," pages 28–32.

Welcome to Gathering 10 of *Heart to Heart*. If we have not already done so, let us circle our chairs around a central table—our focus center. **STOP** Now I will take the articles for our gathering from the supply box and arrange them on the focus center: a cloth covering, a candle and matches (or a lighter), a heart-shaped box, a hand-sized heart, nametags, a wide-edged felt-tip pen, a bell, and envelope #2. **STOP**

Take a moment now to choose a sister's nametag and pin it on her. As you do this, share some words of welcome. When everyone has finished, we will continue. **STOP** ♥

Heartbeat

Note: Play a selection from the "Sing-along" category on pages 202–03 in the "Bibliography of Suggested Music," or play another song, and join in singing. A song about the wind or the Spirit is most appropriate. Then, during "Heartwarmers," softly play "Meditative" music. See page 201 in the "Bibliography of Suggested Music" for selections, or choose other appropriate music.

Heartwarmers

As I light the candle on our focus center, take a deep breath in through your nose. **STOP** Now blow it out through your nose. **STOP** Did you know that the Hebrew word *Ruah* literally means "wind," "spirit," or "breath"? This pause of breath, of getting in touch with God's Spirit, provides us with an opportunity to reflect on how we are in this moment.

As we begin to pay attention to "breath," we learn what we feel, what we think, and what we believe. Such discerning knowledge helps to keep us calm when we are faced with harrowing deadlines and family responsibilities. It provides a simple yet profound way for us to keep in touch with ourselves. ♥

*Note: The person facilitating the following body prayer will not be able to participate fully. The experience will be most effective if the facilitator reads at a relaxed pace, with a soft but strong voice, pausing for at least ten seconds whenever a **STOP** appears.*

Let's begin our gathering by slowing everything down. For this body prayer, it is recommended that you sit cross-legged on the floor. **STOP** If you prefer to sit in a chair, place your feet flat on the floor. **STOP** Free your hands of all objects. **STOP** With your eyes open, focus on the candle as a way to relax. **STOP** Place your hands in front of you in the prayer position. Jesus said, "Blessed are the poor in spirit, for theirs is the king-dom of heaven." **STOP** Lift your chest  and drop your shoulders. **STOP** Slowly and deeply inhale as you extend your arms out, with palms up, to receive your Creator's blessing. Exhale as you bring your arms and hands back to the prayer position.

"Blessed are those who mourn, for they will be comforted." (STOP) Slowly inhale and extend your arms outward again, with palms up, to accept the blessing of Christ. (STOP) Exhale and come back to the prayer position. "Blessed are the meek, for they will inherit the earth." (STOP) Once again, slowly inhale and extend your arms to receive the blessing of the Holy Spirit. (STOP) Now exhale and come back to the prayer position. (STOP) Stay for a moment in the prayer position. (STOP) Feel the breath, *Ruah,* deep within you. Exhale through your nose. (STOP)

Be open to sighs and other sounds that emerge. (STOP)

Place your hands palms down on your knees. (STOP) Close your eyes and give yourself permission to go deeper. (STOP) Take another deep breath in. (STOP) This time, breathe out one word that names something you mourn or fear. Release anger, judgmentalism, or compulsiveness. (STOP) Say no to this behavior or feeling. Make this place and time safe and peaceful—a time of blessing. (STOP)

Sitting up straight, with shoulders back, place your hands on your abdomen with fingers spread. (STOP) Feel your body breathe in its own rhythm. (STOP) "Blessed are those who hunger and thirst for righteousness, for they will be filled." Tell yourself that it is all right to experience fully what you need right now. Move your hands up to your ribs. (STOP) Feel your breath. (STOP) Allow the unimportant to drift away. Place your hands back on your knees. (STOP) Invite yourself to rest. (STOP)

Relax your neck, bending it first to one side (STOP) and then the other. (STOP) Return your head to the center. (STOP) Feel the tension escape from the back of your head through the front of your face. (STOP) Feel the tightness go out from your eyes, eyebrows, cheeks, mouth, and jaw. (STOP) "Blessed are the merciful, for they will receive mercy."

With your hands still on your knees, hold onto your knees. (STOP) Lift your head and chest up. (STOP) Inhale and arch your back backward slightly. (STOP) Exhale as you round your back, pulling your head and chin down. (STOP) Lean back. (STOP) Return to center. (STOP) Imagine God's gentle presence flowing through you—through the back of your neck and down to the base of your spine to your buttocks, (STOP) through your thighs and calves, (STOP) through your heels and into your toes. (STOP) Again, still holding onto your knees, lift your head and chest up. (STOP) Inhale and arch backward slightly. (STOP) Exhale as you round your back, pulling your head and chin down. (STOP) Repeat again: Inhale and arch back. (STOP) Exhale and round down. (STOP)

Interlace your fingers and place them palms down on top of your head.(STOP) Press your elbows back.(STOP) Turn your hands upward.(STOP) Stretch your hands and arms over your head. (STOP) "Blessed are the pure in heart, for they will see God." Return your hands to your knees. (STOP) Again, interlace your fingers and place them palms down on top of your head. (STOP) Press your elbows back. (STOP) Turn your hands upward. (STOP) Stretch your hands and arms over your head. (STOP) Arch your back slightly. (STOP) "Blessed are the peacemakers, for they will be called children of God." Return your hands to your knees.(STOP)

Place your right hand on your left knee and your left hand behind your back, palm flat on the floor. (STOP) Look and twist to your left. (STOP) Increase your twist to the left as you are comfortable and hold. (STOP) On your left, place all that binds you—all that holds you back from being the blessed woman God intends. (STOP) Return to the center. (STOP) Now place your left hand on your right knee and your right hand behind your back, palm flat on the floor. (STOP) Look and twist to your right. (STOP) Increase your twist to the right as you are comfortable and hold. (STOP) On your right, receive the blessings from God that are yours to keep. (STOP) Return to the center. (STOP)

With your hands on your legs, place your feet straight out in front of you. Bend your knees slightly if this is more comfortable.(STOP) With your hands on your legs, stretch forward as far as you can comfortably. (STOP)

Perhaps you remember the snow angels you made as a child. Lie on your back with your head on the floor and knees bent. (STOP) Put your hands at your sides, palms up. (STOP) Now bend your arms at the elbows and slide your arms along the floor so that your hands are touching your shoulders. Hold. (STOP) Slide your hands back to your side. (STOP) Slowly do this motion two more times. (STOP)

Lower your knees and lie flat on the floor, completely relaxed. (STOP) Jesus said those who are weary and heavy with burdens may come to him and he will give them rest. Jesus invites you to be just as you are.

Relax your feet. Completely relax. (STOP) Relax your legs and hips. Completely relax.(STOP) Relax your buttocks and abdomen. Completely relax. (STOP) Relax your lower back. Completely relax.(STOP) Relax your middle torso. Completely relax. (STOP) You are wonderfully made. You are created in God's image.

Relax your chest and upper back. Completely relax. (STOP) Relax your hands and wrists. Completely, totally relax. (STOP) Relax your forearms and elbows. Completely relax. (STOP) Relax your upper arms and shoulders. (STOP) Trust this moment of your Creator to *be* and not *do.* Trust and obey.

Relax your neck, head, and face. Completely relax. (STOP) Daughter, beloved of God, you are relaxed—completely relaxed. Repeat in your heart over and over: "I am God's beloved." (STOP)

Take a deep breath in through your nose. (STOP) When you are ready, allow God's Spirit to breathe into your heart. Accept and welcome the blessings of the Christ Spirit, who dwells within you. (STOP) Invite the Holy Spirit to guide you to what you need. (STOP) Now breathe out a word that affirms what you feel—perhaps *peace, relaxed,* or *love.* (STOP) Say yes to this affirmation. (STOP) Notice all the feelings that are present. (STOP) Welcome feelings that lie just below the surface. (STOP) Breathe into your feelings with acceptance. (STOP)

Continue for a few moments more to complete this journey. (STOP) Slowly open your eyes. (STOP) Remain on your back as you wiggle your fingers and toes. (STOP) Rock your hips. (STOP) Bend your knees and slowly hug them to your chest. (STOP) Roll onto your side and sit up. (STOP) When you are ready, return your attention to the room and return to your seat in the circle, remaining rested and assured. (STOP) ♥

Repeat after me this teaching of Jesus: (STOP)

I give you a new commandment, (STOP)
>**that you love one another, (STOP)**
>**just as I have loved you, . . . (STOP)**
>**By this everyone will know that you are my disciples. (STOP)**
>>>>>*—John 13:34-35, adapted*

A Heart-Centered Story

The Quest of the Woman in Search of Her Heart

Chapter 10

In Chapter 9, Questa wrote a letter to Sage about the difficulties she experienced when she returned to work. Questa wanted to use her new spiritual learnings at the office, but she found that all is not sweetness and light. Even so, as she began to treat each employee as a person of sacred worth, worthy of her time and care, she grew in self-understanding. Today Questa writes to Sage about family matters. Read the letter slowly and thoughtfully.

Dear Sage,

It hasn't been a full two weeks yet, and I've already eaten my way to the back of the refrigerator. I've even devoured the jar of dill pickles. That is what I call desperation! The eating? It's an old habit. I was fortifying my resolve as I got ready to take on my family. ♥

Please understand that our parents loved each other in a quiet fashion. We, like most children, thought of Mom and Dad as asexual, but somehow they bore a boy and two girls whom they treasured—a mystery to us.

Let me tell you what I remember most about my father. Dad was a true extrovert. Right up until the time of his death, he enjoyed sports cars, a day out on the boat, and an evening of laughter with friends. He believed the world had become too rational, had stopped trusting in miracles as much as it should. He once voiced his wonderment that he had raised a child so rational in her decision making. I was the serious, responsible type. With Mom's nervous condition and me being the oldest girl, responsibilities just seemed to fall on me. ♥

My brother lives in California. My sister's house is only a two-hour drive from me, but it might as well be in Timbuktu. As children, we witnessed constant dissension among our parents' siblings; we swore that would never be us. It isn't. Instead, we have become strangers to one another. ♥

Then, one day not long ago, we were together again. We agreed to come together to lay our father's gravestone, one of his last requests. It was something I thought I really wanted to do. Being a responsible person, I felt it was my duty. The chilly air was unexpected. My sweater offered little buffer against the east wind. *What was taking the cemetery guy so long to bring the marker?* I wondered. The three of us stood silently, careful not to step on what represented Dad—a badly seeded spot on the ground. I shivered. No one spoke. Afterward, we agreed to go to a nearby coffee shop to thaw out. ♥

Then something changed. I couldn't pinpoint exactly what it was or how it happened. I blurted out a question. I asked my brother about the unspeakable—Vietnam.

I vividly remember the day he arrived home. It was a Saturday. The family home smelled like holiday company—a unique blend of chocolate chips and ammonia. We each had our own way of waiting. I'd been passing the time memorizing lines for the junior class play. ♥

That evening, my big brother walked through the door in his uniform, hugging each one of us as if there would be no tomorrow. He was one of the lucky ones. His position as a supply agent kept him on the border, out of the combat. He brought gifts for everyone. I listened to him with every fiber of my being as people and places sprang to life. Between the lines hung the loneliness—and a deep, deep sadness over a Vietnamese woman he had loved and left.

Now, twenty years later, I asked again. Tears welled up in the eyes of my six-foot-two-inch tall brother. He told us how they had met over a soda, how she had given solace to a scared eighteen-year-old boy. In his final act of love, my brother had left the woman all his money, hoping beyond hope that she would escape the bonds of prostitution placed on her by her family. He hadn't told anyone about giving her his money because he thought his comrades would think he was foolish. ♥

Now he told us, "For a long time, I would look down a street and see her there. I'd begin working on a report, and I'd find myself writing about her. I'm not even sure how I got home that week. Somehow the planes and buses carried me, yet I barely remember the miles going by. So here I am, still walking around with another person inside of me." ♥

Then my sister told her story of being tangled with an abusive husband, an unplanned pregnancy, and little money to smooth the way. Finally, I shared that I too am looking for my heart. We cried together.

But our time together wasn't all tears. We also laughed. We retold the bittersweet, funny, and tragic stories of our childhood—like the time our baby sister cut her chin with her fork while eating spaghetti, and we discovered it only after washing the sauce off her face. And the time Dad brought home Cassius Clay boxing gloves; I forfeited three teeth to my brother in the second round. And we laughed until we cried as we recalled the time my sister's tongue was stuck to the frozen metal spout after church. ♥

Sage, telling our stories expressed messages that we could not have communicated any other way. We discovered in their magic the home-woven tales of our lives that continue to knit us together as family. My siblings' stories of courage, humor, and wisdom now illuminate my path. ♥

In our final minutes together, with triumphant hugs goodbye, I saw it laid out. For a split second, celebration merged past, present, and future into a cohesive whole. Each one of their stories became my story. Through them I gained a new understanding of the past and present to carry me into my future. ♥

So, I've learned a few things from my family in this search for my heart. Obviously, I've learned that it pays to risk with people you love and care about. Second, the real test is not how much I want to do something, but how much love is a part of what I want to do. And third, when I'm anxious about the future, it is a sign that I may be out of touch with God's presence. In contrast, confidence in the future based on trust in God frees me to live fully in the present. ♥

I tend to shut out my family—those whom I most need to hear. I now see that if I can identify those to whom I am least drawn and can make a special effort to listen to them attentively, I will find clues to my heart. Prayerful listening may be the most important aspect of finding my heart. ♥

It is through the stories in my life that God is trying to tell me the things I need to know. My actions, my choices, the paths I take—all these hold clues to whom I am becoming.

I ask you to continue to hold me gently in prayer. I pray for you, too, sister. May this message find you in peace.

Love and Blessings,

Questa

To be continued ... ♥

Sacred Story Bible Study

Note: If this is a thirty-minute gathering, or if your group will not be doing the Bible study together for another reason, move on to the next

section. Take some time this week to read and reflect on the Sacred Story.

As we use the "Praying the Scripture" method of "Sacred Story Bible Study" today, listen once again to the wise words of Madame Guyon, whose instructions on Scripture and prayer are as relevant today as they were over 280 years ago.

If there are more than five women in our full group, we will divide into small circles of three to five by choosing women whom we know the least. We will space our groups around the room and circle our chairs so that we are sitting knee to knee. Each group will need to choose a facilitator, who will guide her group through the entire Sacred Story exercise. We will remain in quiet reflection and prayer until all of the groups are finished. 🛑 ♥

Praying the Scripture

Note: The small group facilitator begins reading here.

Turn in your journal to page 81, "Praying the Scripture Sacred Story Bible Study: Glass Houses." I will read the wise words of Madame Guyon, which appear in italics, followed by the directions, which appear in bold print. After reading each segment, I will pause so that we may work through the process together. 🛑

Note: Follow the directions on pages 81–84 in your journal to complete the study. When finished, return quietly to the larger circle and fast from speech until everyone has completed the study. 🛑 ♥

You've Got to Have Heart

Now I will open the second envelope given to Questa by Sage and distribute one piece of paper to each person. 🛑 Let us receive the message together by reading it aloud. Rather than share our thoughts with one another, let us remain silent as we prepare for a time of quiet journaling. *Note: Lead the group in reading the message aloud, which also may be found on page 85 of From the Heart Journal: A Personal Prayer Journal for Women. Then the next reader continues.* 🛑 ♥

From the Heart Journal:
A Personal Prayer Journal for Women

Turn in your journal to page 86, "A Letter from God to Me." During the next ten minutes, we will fast from speech and follow the instructions on the journal page to write our letters. I will let you know when time is up. When we come back together, we will not share our letters but will proceed with the closing prayer ritual. _Note: Ring the bell after ten minutes._ ♥

A Hearty Goodbye

Gathering 11 will take place on _(date/s)_ at _(time/s and place/s)_. _Note: If you are using the multiple groups format, explain that participants may attend any scheduled gathering. If the group needs to discuss meeting dates, times, and places, do so now._ 🛑

In spite of our wordiness, 80 percent of our communication is nonverbal. The subtle signs and body signals you display tell people about your true self—who you are, and even what mood you are in.

Following a group prayer, we will pause for one minute of silent reflection and prayer. I will give you a signal indicating that time is up. You then are invited to rise in silence and show a nonverbal sign of gratitude, such as a hug or a hearty handshake, to the person on your right and the person on your left.

With this in mind, let us now pray together the closing prayer. 🛑

Gracious God,
> **Not out of conceit, but out of concern**
> > **we pray for ourselves.**
> **Fill us with compassion and gentle ways.**
> **Where we are false, purify us;**
> > **where we are faithless, direct us;**

155

where there is anything that is wayward, convict us.
Where we are right, strengthen us;
   where we are in need, provide for us;
   where we are divided within ourselves, reunite us;
   for the love of Jesus Christ, our teacher and savior. Amen.

Note: After one minute of silence, ring the bell to indicate that it is time to express silent gratitude to your sisters on the left and right. When all have done this, ring the bell a second time and continue. **(STOP)**

Now close your eyes. **(STOP)** Inhale one deep, long breath. **(STOP)** Hold it. Now blow it out. **(STOP)**

Remember to take off your nametag and place it on the focus center as you leave. As I extinguish the candle, reflect on these words:

The peace of God,
      the love of Christ,
            and the blessings of the Spirit go with you. **(STOP)**

Gathering 11

Heartbeat

Note: Play a selection from the "Music for Movement" category on pages 201–02 of the "Bibliography of Suggested Music," or another appropriate song, to get everyone "tuned in" for this Heart to Heart gathering.

Circle of Hearts

Note: One woman begins the gathering by reading aloud to the group. Read slowly and thoughtfully, pausing as appropriate and as directed by this symbol, ⬟, to allow time for reflection and response. For more-detailed reminders on how to open and conduct a Heart to Heart gathering, refer to "Getting Started," pages 28–32.

We have gathered here with a very special purpose. As a community of believers, we come together to celebrate the Creator, who made us women full of personal integrity, with a passion for life, and with powerful choices. If we have not already done so, let us circle our chairs around a central table—our focus center. ⬟ Now I will take the articles for our gathering from the supply box and arrange them on the focus center: a cloth covering; a candle and matches (or a lighter); a heart-shaped box; a hand-sized heart; nametags; a wide-edged felt-tip pen; a bell; bread wrapped in a cloth napkin; three candles—yellow, blue, and red—to be placed around the larger candle to create a triangle; envelope #3; and copies of the "Participant's Comment Form." ⬟

Come and take your nametag in the order of your birth year. We'll start with those born before 1940. Anyone? ⬟ How about before 1945?

157

STOP 1950? **STOP** 1955? **STOP** *Note: Continue in this manner until every-one has retrieved her nametag. After everyone has returned to her seat, proceed with the gathering.* **STOP**

Heartbeat

Note: For the prayer ritual in "Heartwarmers," which follows the lighting of the candles, choose a selection from the "Meditative" cate-gory on page 201 in the "Bibliography of Suggested Music," or choose other appropriate music. It is important that the selection not be a famil-iar song that may distract anyone's thoughts.

Heartwarmers

During this gathering, we celebrate the end of our blindness and the beginning of our awakening and new learnings. I light the center can-dle to celebrate the sensual, creative, caring woman who is a source of life to herself as well as to others. **STOP** We acknowledge, honor, and affirm God's work and transformation in each woman here.

I light this warm yellow candle to welcome our sisters and the Spirit's direction. **STOP**

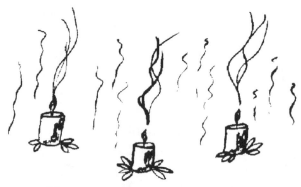

I light this true blue candle to create a sacred space where we may gather safely as we seek support. **STOP**

I light this passion red candle to open the paths of creativity that lead to healing. **STOP**

Join me in saying aloud the following:

We light these candles to celebrate the diversity of our gathered lives: yellow, blue, and red for direction, support, and healing. We are thankful. ♥

Note: The woman facilitating the following storytelling may not be able to participate fully. Read slowly, picturing the scenes in your own mind. Pause as often as you feel appropriate.

You may sit in your chair or get comfortable on the floor. I invite you to close your eyes and open your imagination. Imagine that Sage, the wise one, has invited you to step away from your "too much to do" syndrome and go for a walk. To prepare yourself for this walk, take three long, deep breaths.

Sage tells you to go to the water's edge, where she will meet you. As you wait by the water in the late day's light, take your shoes off and dip your feet into the cool, clear water. You drift dreamily. Hear the song of the birds. Smell the sweet spring air. You wash in the water and then lie in the sand, which still holds a hint of warmth from the day's sun.

Now you sit up and watch the sun setting directly before you. You are aware of the peacefulness that surrounds you. The sun dips its golden edge slowly into the water. Inch by inch it descends to the other side of the earth. The sun's glow of orange, pink, and yellow flutters across the water toward you. You smell the scent of the water carried by the breeze.

In the distance you see a woman walking along the beach toward you. She comes and stands next to you. The last of the sun's rays casts a golden path over the water and onto the sand. She takes you by the hand, and you walk together in the warm, glowing light...and you talk.

She says she has brought a gift for you. It is the gift of prayer that brings light. It shines like a moonbeam in her hand. She places it upon your head like a crown. With it, she tells you, you will be able to cast aside whatever keeps you wounded, saps your energy, and sucks life out of you. With it, she tells you, you will find light for the way. She reminds you of the light that Jesus spoke of when he said, "If your eye is healthy, your whole body will be full of light" (*Matthew 6:22*). With it, you have a light that allows you to be present to yourself and fully awake to life. You see clearly what is important and has value. With it, you not only grow in love, but as Jesus promised, you also become love.

There is a long silence. She asks, "Why do you refuse to come home to your heart?" The question lingers as you listen to the rhythm of the water singing your name.

She tells you she also brings news of a second gift, but it is not her gift. It is the gift of the Holy Spirit, who lives within you. Through the Spirit, you will discover the faith that opens the eyes of the heart to the presence of the Divine Light. Somewhere, from deep within, you know that all you need to do is accept the gift.

Then, as if on signal, the two of you face the ocean and lift your arms, saluting truth and surrendering to love.

As a parting blessing, the wise one embraces you in her arms. Then you step out of her embrace and walk alone along the moonlit path.

As you walk back, you notice changes in the night sky and recognize the changes you have experienced. You are at home with your heart. As you open your eyes, you feel cleansed and refreshed. ♥

A Heart-Centered Story

The Quest of the Woman in Search of Her Heart

Chapter 11

In the last chapter, Questa wrote to Sage about her "family reunion." She reluctantly traveled to join her siblings in a final farewell to their father, only to discover that childhood stories of courage, humor, and wisdom would illumine her path. Today we find Questa writing yet another letter to Sage. Remember to read the letter slowly and *thoughtfully.*

Dear Sage,

My Great Auntie used to say to me when I complained, "Child, the Lord won't give you more than you can bear!" Her saying may be true, but I've discovered that God doesn't give me some of these burdens I lug around. I put them on myself. And "myself" needs to shake them off! So I'm busy shaking—shaking loose children who can manage without me, shaking "to do's" from my list, shedding goals that no longer are in keeping with who I am. I didn't get to be a woman-who-does-too-much all by myself. I was painstakingly trained. This shaking-off thing is putting my life in perspective. I simply have stopped carrying those worries, and I am beginning to live my life. *I do not need to suffer* to feel totally alive. ♥

I feel a thousand pounds lighter. I wake up, and I don't feel lost any-more. Situations that once would have overwhelmed me no longer have power over me. With this new sense of freedom, I discover that I can take on larger roles as my heart expands. So I widen my circle. I volunteer at the city shelter and find myself tutoring a child in reading. Next, on a whim, I drop by Mrs. Rice's house. Newly widowed, she seems genuinely pleased to share a cup of coffee. She says something about how lonely it is eating all your meals alone. I register for those painting classes I've been wanting to take for eons. I even take care of myself: I actually have scheduled exercise time on my calendar. ♥

But my new word for the week is *grace*. Grace is a special kind of forgiveness that says, "I'll do the best I can and leave the rest to God." I live with grace for myself and others. I recognize that I don't have to do it all, all by myself. And did you know that chaos *always* happens? It's not because I'm doing something wrong. There are always wrench-es thrown into the works. I only exercised once last week, and I wasn't able to go to the shelter for a couple of weeks because of other com-mitments with friends. But it's all right. I no longer get uptight, thinking that I have to do everything perfectly—or do it all. I am able to rest, knowing that God is ultimately in charge—and I don't have to be. What a relief! I always want to be God's "work in progress." ♥

Remember when you told me the story about Jesus and the sisters, Mary and Martha? Mary sits right down to talk with Jesus while Martha is doing the housekeeping. When Martha complains, Jesus tells her that Mary has made the better choice.

I didn't get the point of the story at the time. Now I see that perhaps Mary is not afraid to sit in God's grace, to be herself, to be abundant in life, to live the extraordinary in the midst of the ordinary. Mary boldly steps into the unknown and takes a seat. She dares to live in the miracle of the ordinary. I imagine Mary as a woman open to the wonders of life. ♥

Martha, on the other hand, lives with the illusion of control. Perhaps, like me, she is hiding within the order of her house while missing the "better part" of life. I like to think that after Jesus' talk with her, she lets go of some of her control issues in order to grab hold of the promise. I picture her anguishing through the dark night of letting go. Then, like me, maybe she says goodbye to those pieces that no longer fit, the stuff that no longer works. Perhaps she lets go of the fantasies of what she thought her life would be—and who she thought God was. Maybe Martha was living in the tension that comes from feeling pressured by the dreary repetitiveness of everyday chores; and maybe she forgot her own design, just as I forgot mine. Maybe she started seeing only the ordinary—"This is all there is. This is the best and worst there is. This is it." ♥

At my father's memorial service, the eulogist spoke of his "expansive heart." I think I understand now what she meant. My newly recovered heart has begun to expand, taking on the ways of the Spirit: love, joy, peace, patience, kindness, generosity, faithfulness, gentleness, and self-control. All my life people have been telling me *about* God. But with your encouragement and direction, I have *experienced* God—not in loud, flamboyant ways, but in the still, small voice that Wisdom speaks. With new eyes to see, and new ears to hear, I now have a spiritual intimacy with God. ♥

All that I've written lays the groundwork for what I am about to tell you.

I went to church this morning. That in itself is not earth-shattering. Going to church hasn't felt good for a long time, because I thought you had to be dressed up to go, both on the outside and on the inside. Those spotless white gloves of a little six-year-old girl on Easter morning became the symbol of my expectations. I stopped enjoying worship when I saw I could no longer be perfect, could no longer be always good. ♥

The service is proceeding as usual when something strange happens. I am walking forward, hesitantly, to the Communion table when the sweetest little girl, about six years old, scoots up next to me, reaches up, and takes my hand. I'm sure she sees the startled look on my face, but when I look into her eyes I know this is as it is to be. We walk on, my hand in hers, to the front. ♥

At the table, I find my name, my place, and my story. I meet Jesus at the table as he said I would, and I remember who I am. I meet him there with my ordinary life and broken heart, with my hunger and emptiness. When the server places the bread gently in my palm, she calls my name. Then she says, "The Body of Christ, given for you." I look into her eyes and see the Christ. ♥

As I eat the given bread, I admit my hunger. In that moment, I am convinced that my overeating, the binges I often lapse into, point to a frightening emptiness that runs deep and wide within me. I join myself to other persons in their hunger and acknowledge my dependence upon God and others for the necessities of life.

Then, looking into the cup, I know that I am part of something deeper and richer than my own limited world. In that moment of illumination, I am shown that my hungers need not go unsatisfied. This God gives bread and "wine"—tangible, visible symbols of love for the deserts of life. And as I say "Amen," I admit the presence of a gift, a gift that fills my need. Just think! God invites me to the head of the table! ♥

Imagine—God enduring my bad table manners all these years so that I may now look beyond the chaos of today to sit at God's table forever. In that moment of bread and cup, all became one. I am able to give thanks for all that is and has been and is yet to be in my life.* ♥

Tonight, when I opened the third envelope, it seemed empty. I thought that there had been some mistake, or that maybe I had lost the letter.

Note: Move to the focus center, open envelope #3, and give one of the small mirrors inside it to each woman now. Then continue reading. 🛑

I looked a second time and found a small mirror. I peer into the reflective surface. Then I see it: my heart. As I gaze at my heart, a light radiates from the center, as from a precious diamond. And I feel my own heart melt around it. I sit there for a long spell, laughing and crying at the same time, and I understand.

I sense that you understand too.*

Questa

To be continued... ♥

Sacred Story Bible Study

Note: If this is a thirty-minute gathering, or if your group will not be doing the Bible study together for another reason, move on to the next section. Take some time this week to read and reflect on the Sacred Story.

Today we will be using the Imagine This! method of Sacred Story Bible Study. If there are more than five women in our full group, we will divide into small circles of three to five by choosing women whom we know the least. We will space our groups around the room and circle our chairs so that we are sitting knee to knee. Each group will need to choose a facilitator, who will guide her group through the entire Sacred Story exercise. We will remain in quiet reflection and prayer until all of the groups are finished. 🛑 ♥

Imagine This!

Note: The small group facilitator begins reading here.

Turn in your journal to page 88, "Imagine This! Sacred Story Bible Study: Sister, Sister." In this exercise we will read the Sacred Story three times. After each reading, we will be instructed to close our eyes and use our imaginations to discover the story's meaning for us. I will read each step, pausing as indicated so that we may follow the instructions and reflect on the Scripture. 🛑 *Note: Follow the directions on pages 88–89 in your journal to complete the study. When finished, quietly return to the larger circle and fast from speech until everyone has com pleted the study.* 🛑 ♥

*Questa's story of receiving the Lord's Supper was inspired by the book *Sunday Dinner: The Lord's Supper and the Christian Life,* by William H. Willimon, Upper Room Books, 1981. Some of the words used are his phrasings.

Heartbeat

Note: Play any "Meditative" music selection of your choice. See page 201 in the "Bibliography of Suggested Music," or choose another appropriate song.

As the music plays, I will pass the bread from our focus center around the circle. When the bread comes to you, break off a piece and serve the sister on your right. As you place the piece of bread in her palm, say her name. Take time to look into each other's hearts as the person receiving the bread eats it. I will begin.

Note: You will begin by serving the sister on your right, but you will not be served until last. After you have been served, return the bread to the focus center and continue the gathering. 🛑 ♥

From the Heart Journal: A Personal Prayer Journal for Women

Now, turn in your journal to pages 90–91, "Paths to My Heart." Follow the instructions on these pages. We will fast from speech for ten minutes while we write. I will let you know when time is up. 🛑 *Note: Ring the bell when ten minutes have passed.* 🛑

Between now and the next time we meet, you will want to continue recording in your journal the paths you have taken to your heart. You will be invited to share some of your learnings from this journal page at our concluding gathering. ♥

A Hearty Goodbye

Gathering 12 will take place on *(date/s)* at *(time/s and place/s)*. *Note: If you are using the multiple groups format, explain that participants may attend any scheduled gathering. If the group needs to discuss meeting dates, times, and places, do so now.* 🛑

Note: The person facilitating will not be able to participate in the following exercise. Instead, stand in the center of the circle. Pause at least ten seconds at each 🛑 .

Stand and form a circle. 🛑 Your hands should be free of any objects.

Hear these words from the Sacred Story. Repeat each line after me: **STOP**

"Martha, Martha, you are worried and distracted by many things; STOP
there is need of only one thing. STOP
Mary has chosen the better part, STOP
which will not be taken away from her." STOP

—Luke 10:41b-42

Like Mary and Martha, who were friends of Jesus, we may choose to worry and be distracted or we may choose "the better part," which no one can take from us. Jesus wants us to have this "better part." ♥

You are standing in a circle. You are part of the circle. Reach out and take the hands of the women who stand on either side of you. <u>*Note: The reader steps into the center of the circle.*</u> **STOP** Feel the collective power of the women in this circle. Breathe together a deep, lingering breath. **STOP**

As you take this breath, your eyes are opened to the reality that you are relaxed and energized, ready to move on in your journey. As you breathe with these women, you breathe with all God's creation.

As we prepare to leave, let us share the ancient blessing of Christians. I say to you, *"The peace of the Lord be with you."* You respond, **"And also with you."** **STOP**

Share these ancient words of peace with at least three others before you leave. Remember to take off your nametag and place it on the focus center. Also, please take a copy of the "Participant's Comment Form," complete it as you have time, and bring it with you to our final gathering. I extinguish the candle as we prepare to leave. **STOP**

Gathering 12

Heartbeat

Note: Play warm, reflective music as you gather. Choose from the "Meditative" selections on page 201 in the "Bibliography of Suggested Music," or choose other appropriate music. If you wish, you may continue playing the music throughout "Circle of Hearts" and "Heartwarmers." Be sure to keep the volume low so that you may hear one another speak.

Circle of Hearts

Note: One woman begins the gathering by reading aloud to the group. Read slowly, allowing time for reflection as appropriate. For more detailed reminders on how to open and conduct a Heart to Heart *gathering, refer to "Getting Started," pages 28–32.*

Welcome to our twelfth and final gathering of *Heart to Heart*. We end our journey together as we began, with a heart-centered ritual. If we have not already done so, let us circle our chairs around a central table—our focus center. **STOP** Now I will take the articles for our gathering from the supply box and arrange them on the focus center: a cloth covering, a candle and matches (or a lighter), a heart-shaped box, a hand-sized heart, nametags, a wide-edged felt-tip marker, a bell, a colorful ribbon archway, and heart necklaces—one for each of us. **STOP**

I now invite you to place on the focus center an item that is representative of you—perhaps an earring, your keys, your watch, your scarf, or even a shoe. (STOP)

Come and choose the nametag of someone you didn't know very well—if at all—when you first began attending *Heart to Heart*. This woman has become a friend. Pin her nametag on her. When everyone has returned to her seat, we will continue. (STOP)

Heartwarmers

When we began *Heart to Heart* many weeks ago, we were not always comfortable talking about spiritual matters. Many of us tended to keep religion at the head level. We found it disquieting to talk about God and our faith where they touch us personally—at the heart level. As I light the candle on our focus center, we thank God for leading us to this special time and place. (STOP) This candle symbolizes our decision to set this time apart. We want to be aware of who we are and how we live as daughters of God.

Let's say together Mother Teresa's prayer about strangers and friends.

> **Lord, open our eyes,**
> **that we may see you in our**
> **brothers and sisters.**
> **Lord open our ears,**
> **that we may hear the cries**
> **of the hungry,**
> **the cold,**
> **the frightened,**
> **the oppressed.**
> **Lord, open our hearts,**
> **that we may love each other**
> **as you love us.**

Renew in us your Spirit.
Lord, free us
and make us one. *♥

Our teacher Jesus says,

"Do not let your hearts be troubled. Believe in God, believe also in me. In my Father's house there are many dwelling places. If it were not so, would I have told you that I go to prepare a place for you? And if I go and prepare a place for you, I will come again and will take you to myself, so that where I am, there you may be also." —John 14:1-3

Now let us quiet ourselves as we feel our connection to God. ♥
Note: The woman facilitating the following exercise may not be able to participate fully. Read slowly, pausing for at least ten seconds at each **STOP** *.*

Close your eyes and take three deep, relaxing breaths. **STOP** Picture yourself in a room. It is a room of your own. **STOP** What color is the room? **STOP** Picture its size. **STOP** Feel its texture. **STOP** Smell its fragrances. **STOP** What sounds do you hear? Or perhaps it is quiet. **STOP** Now, design the furnishings of the room. **STOP**

Place windows in the room. What do you view from the window? **STOP** Create a space that is open and welcoming. Where are you in this room? **STOP** Become present in this place. Are you sitting or standing? **STOP**

Imagine that you are walking to the window. **STOP** You see a stream of iridescent light become a path. You follow the path. **STOP** The path leads to God. **STOP** Allow yourself to be open and to look deeply into the presence of God. Feel God's warmth dissolve distance and space so that you are standing right in the heart of God. Feel yourself connected with a lifeline to God's divine strength and power. **STOP** Reach out and touch the bands of golden joy, love, and peace. Draw these into yourself. **STOP** Bathe in the warmth for a moment longer. **STOP**

Slowly, the light fades. The shapes and colors of the room return.

You become aware of yourself, yet you do not lose God's presence. You carry that stream of warmth deep within you, in the very core of your being. You remain deeply, intimately bonded. (STOP) Slowly, as you are ready, open your eyes and return your attention to this circle of friends. (STOP) ♥

A Heart-Centered Story

The Quest of the Woman in Search of Her Heart

Chapter 12

In the previous chapter, Questa sent a letter to Sage, telling of her new lightness and grace and her tangible, visible experience of God. While receiving the bread and cup during the Lord's Supper, Questa had recovered her heart. The third envelope from Sage contained a mirror. As Questa gazed at her newly found heart, a light radiated from the center, as from a precious diamond, and she felt her own heart melt around it. In this last chapter of our story, Questa returns to pay Sage a final visit. Remember to read slowly and thoughtfully.

The room is still.

"Sage? It's Questa. Where are you?"

No answer. Questa has traveled the distance to Sage's home once again. Somehow, this time, the journey did not seem as long. Now she wanders from room to room, expecting her friend to be just around the next corner. She goes out the back door and into the garden. There Questa rests on the bench where she and her friend shared long hours of conversation and coffee. The gardens are as pleasing and fragrant as ever.

Then Questa's eye catches a fluttering piece of white paper at the other end of the bench. It is secured by a conch shell. The note reads,

Questa,
    Somehow I knew you might come. I've gone on my annual hike into the mountains. It is time to be alone. I am no

longer needed here. In you, God's work will travel on. Enjoy the house and gardens.

Love and Blessings,
Sage ♥

Questa's heart sinks. She wants so much to thank her mentor for helping her find her heart. It is a debt she can never repay. She moves to the pool of water and dips her fingers once more to feel the coolness. In that moment, she senses that Sage's presence is still there in the garden with her. It always will be. The silence speaks eloquently—two spirits joined together. And, in that awesome realization, Questa presses her pen to her journal and writes: ♥

> Finding and listening to my heart,
> > finding out who I am
> > and who God is,
> > have not been simple.
> It took time for the chatter to quiet down;
> > but then, in the silence of "not doing,"
> > in simply "being,"
> > I began to know what I felt.
> Even now, if I listen really hard
> > and hear what is offered,
> > the Spirit is my guide. ♥

She reads her reflection aloud, as if Sage were her audience. It feels strange to be reading aloud to someone who isn't there. The phrases are simple, elegant, and from the heart—a reflection of their precious time together. Losing and then finding her heart helped Questa recognize the cycle of life and death. Part of her had to die so that something new could be born. Her experience echoes the words of Paul: "It is no longer I who live, but it is Christ who lives in me" (*Galatians 2:20a*). ♥

Questa has been blessed. She found a mentor and guide who affirmed her and helped her see the vast possibilities of life. The search caused her to look deeply and find the Christ who gives meaning to the faith that now lives within her. The journey to her heart has been arduous.

But now that she has found her path, she sees that she can share it with others, offering the gift of herself living within the heart of God. ♥

Questa takes a deep breath; and, as she exhales, a smile of contentment forms on her lips. With new assurance she walks back into the kitchen. Out of habit, she begins to make a pot of coffee. She will drink a cup of blessing to Sage, wherever her mentor may be. ♥

As Questa spoons in the freshly ground beans, she hears a hesitant knock at the front door. She isn't even sure she's heard it. Perhaps it was just a branch hitting against the house. She plugs in the coffeepot. The knock comes again, slightly louder. When she opens the door, Questa finds a woman, looking disheveled and ill at ease.

"I've traveled a long way to get here," the woman says haltingly. "I was given this address by a friend." The woman shows Questa a now-tattered piece of paper. "She said you might be able to help me." ♥

"Sage, the woman who lives here, isn't home," Questa responds.

"But you are here," the young woman points out pleadingly. "I haven't driven all this way for nothing, have I? My friend said that there was a woman here who could give me some advice." There is an awkward silence. ♥

"Sage and I are friends," Questa finally offers. "She helped me when I was struggling. I learned a lot from her." There is another awkward pause as they both stare at each other. ♥

"Perhaps I shouldn't have come. I didn't mean to waste your time," blurts out the young woman.

"Have some coffee with me," says Questa, showing the woman to a seat. She pours the rich brew into the earthenware cups. "You've had a busy life?" Questa asks.

"All my days," the young woman replies.

"Why?" Questa asks.

"What do you mean, 'Why?' " the woman quizzes back.

"Why have you been so busy?" Questa clarifies. ♥

"I thought that was the way to make it all work. I tried self-help books without any result. Therapy helped some, but it couldn't heal my pain of growing up in a family that has been deeply wounded for generations. It is not as though I don't have a good job and family, so why am I now feeling lost? Why can't I figure out what life is about?"

"You sound as though you've lost your heart," Questa muses aloud, as she recalls the words Sage spoke at their first meeting.

"How did you know? It feels just like that. It's as though I have this big empty space right where my heart used to be. Can you help me?" ♥

Questa feels awkward, but she moves forward toward the woman. *Can I help her?* she wonders. Questa has learned a few things from Sage about how to be a good friend and guide, about mutual respect, about letting herself be known deeply by someone else and finding herself in the process. Being a spiritual mentor is about being a midwife rather than a healer; it is not a matter of giving answers but of suggesting directions to explore. In her own journey, Questa has learned how to affirm and support another. Most important, Questa sees that her primary work as one who would be a spiritual friend is to help others, even as she remains mindful of herself; she is to pay attention to the response of God's presence in their lives. ♥

Questa yearns to say yes—to share the light of Christ that she herself has found with another, offering her own blessings from the heart.

Questa turns and looks the woman straight in the eye. "I can't tell you how to find your heart," she says. "Only you know where it is. No one can make the journey for you. Only you know the way back to your heart. But I can walk with you."
The End . . .

and another beginning . . .

Sacred Story Bible Study

Note: If this is a thirty-minute gathering, or if your group will not be doing the Bible study together for another reason, move on to the next section. Take some time this week to read and reflect on the Sacred Story.

For our final "Sacred Story Bible Study," we will remain together as a full circle as we use the Responsive Listening method. Together we have sought to discern what God is saying to us. It is appropriate for us to conclude our journey together in this way. I will serve as the facilitator for the entire study.

Responsive Listening

For this exercise, we will read the account of a final meeting between Jesus' friend Mary, two angels, and Jesus. The scene takes place after Jesus' death. Turn in your journal to page 92, "Responsive Listening Sacred Story Bible Study: Seeing Jesus!" (STOP)

 will read the directions, pausing after each step so that we may work through the process together. (STOP)

Note: Follow the directions on pages 92–94 in your journal to complete the study. When finished, move on to the journaling activity. (STOP) ♥

From the Heart Journal:
A Personal Prayer Journal for Women

Writing in our journals is humbling. We always return to a blank page. The thoughts and feelings we've written in our journals cause us to be honest with God as we go back in our memories, weeding out all that is not authentic. Both the practice of journaling and the practice of writing start deep within; as they cause things to rise to the surface, they reveal our truth. That truth, one hopes, is a word of love wrapped in grace. ♥

Turn now in your journal to page 90, "Paths to My Heart." (STOP) We will be silent for one minute as we each select one of our learnings to share with the group. This may be an insight that has brought growth and transformation during *Heart to Heart*. Then, one at a time, we will share with the group. This will not be a time to give verbal feedback but a time to listen to one another. As we share, we will participate in a closing ceremony to celebrate the journey we have made together. I will give instructions when it is time.

Now, let's fast from speech for one minute. I will let you know when time is up. (STOP) *Note: Signal to the group when one minute has passed.* (STOP)

A Hearty Goodbye

Questa's journey continues as she reaches out to another, and so it is with our own journeys. We are a brave group of souls. In reality, friendships with women are **dangerous**, because they help us to identify our common soft spots and tell what we know; **intimate**, because they enable us to reveal our true selves to one another; and **essential**, because they break through our loneliness and connect us to what is important. Let us embrace each of these aspects of friendship now as we listen to one another with open and loving hearts. ♥

For this closing ceremony, we will ask two of the taller members of our group to stand and hold the colorful ribbon-wrapped cord from the focus center over their heads, forming an archway. *Note: Allow time for the women to form the archway now.* 🛑 I will share first. After I have finished, I will pass through the archway. One at a time, each of you will share and then pass through the archway. As each woman passes through, those of us on the other side will welcome her with hugs and signs of congratulation. The woman who passed through the archway before her will place around her neck a heart necklace from the focus center, symbolizing that she has found her own heart. We then will join hands, encircle the woman, and say a brief prayer or  words of blessing before moving on to the next person. When only the two women holding the archway remain, we will ask two other sisters to take their places so that they too may share and pass through. After the last woman has joined the circle, someone in the group may then place a heart necklace around my neck and lead the group in offering a prayer or words of blessing on my behalf. *Note: If you wish, you may say the following blessing for each woman during the ceremony:*

**_(Name)_, you are God's beloved.
May you continue to grow in insight, knowledge, and love. Amen.**

Are there any questions about what we are to do? _Note: Pause for any questions, allowing anyone in the circle to answer._ Then proceed with the ceremony. **STOP**

Let us end our final gathering by saying this prayer of commitment to one another in unison: **STOP**

> **This is my commitment to you, my friends:**
> > **to value your thoughts and feelings,
> > even when they may differ from my own;
> > to be honest with you,
> > but always to blanket honesty in love;
> > to respect and esteem each of you
> > as a person of sacred worth;
> > to listen to you, not only with my head,
> > but primarily with my heart.**
> **This is my commitment to myself:**
> > **to never again allow anyone to trample on my heart,
> > to remain as awake as possible,
> > to continue the struggle**
> > > **with the disciplines of the spiritual journey, and
> > > to be faithful amid the many changes of my life.**

These commitments I make before you and before God.

Heartbeat

Note: After reading aloud the following words, play or sing together a song of your choice. (See the "Bibliography of Suggested Music," pages 200–03, or use other songs.) Or, if you are not using music in your gatherings, simply offer signs of love and appreciation.

Now hear this special blessing to each one of us. As the song plays, or as we sing, let us share signs of love and appreciation, thanking God and one another for the *Heart to Heart* time we've enjoyed together.

Our gathering will end with the song. Feel free to linger and visit if you like. You may take your nametag and heart necklace with you as keepsakes. Please leave your "Participant's Comment Form" on the focus center before you leave, and remember to retrieve the personal item you placed there at the beginning of our gathering. The last person to leave will blow out the candle. **STOP**

Appendix

Equipment and Supplies Checklist

General Equipment and Supplies
- comfortable chairs for participants
- adjustable lighting *(lamps or dimmer-controlled overhead lights)*
- CD or tape player and recorded music *(See the "Bibliography of Suggested Music," pages 200–03, or choose other appropriate music.)*
- piano, guitar, or other instrument for live music *(optional)*
- pencils or pens for all participants
- copies of *Heart to Heart Guidebook* and *From the Heart Journal: A Personal Prayer Journal for Women (one of each for each participant)*
- registration/attendance cards *(optional; see page 192)*

Focus Center
- table
- tablecloth, fabric, and/or scarf to cover table
- pillar candle in attractive holder, or "glass jar candle" with removable lid
- matches or lighter
- hand-sized heart made of glass, wood, or other material
- heart-shaped box made of glass, cardboard, or wood *(Most craft stores and/or craft departments of local discount stores have heart-shaped boxes made of wood or cardboard, which may be painted and decorated attractively. Because the box must be large enough to hold one small wooden heart for each woman, the size of the box is determined by the size of the group—approximately 4" x 4" or 6" x 6".)*
- bell
- other heart symbols *(optional)*
- wide-edged felt-tip markers *(one for every two participants for gathering 1; one thereafter)*
- permanent nametags *(Because these are used over and over at each gathering, use nametag holders made of sturdy plastic or other durable material. You can find these at any office supply store.*

Nametag inserts that may be reproduced, cut apart, and slipped inside the holders are provided on page 191. Or, if you prefer, make your own attractive nametags. Do not use the stick-on type. A stick-on nametag is temporary and communicates that message to the person receiving it. Always keep additional nametags available for new women who may join your gathering.)

Note: All of the preceding items are used at every gathering. Additional materials required for specific gatherings are as follows.

Gathering 1
- small wooden hearts for each woman, approximately two inches *(You can find wooden hearts in craft stores and/or the craft department of your local discount store. Spray paint each heart completely and let it dry. Using a marking pen, paint pen, or paint and brush, inscribe on each heart one word from the word list found on pages 26–27 of From the Heart Journal: A Personal Prayer Journal for Women. Have extras on hand in case new women come to Gathering 2.)*
- suggested music *(See "Heartbeat" suggestions on pages 49, 51)*

Gathering 2
- ten- or twelve-inch taper or candlestick
- suggested music *(See "Heartbeat" suggestions on pages 60–62.)*

Gathering 3
- bowl of potpourri
- suggested music *(See "Heartbeat" suggestions on pages 72–74, 82.)*

Gathering 4
- cloth napkin
- blessing cup *(This is basically a mug. You may purchase a coffee mug painted with hearts, or you may inscribe the words Heart to Heart on a one-color mug, or you even may have a potter create a special mug for your group. Place your blessing cup on the focus center before the gathering begins.)*
- one bottle of flavored water *(Purchase flavored water from the grocery store, chill, and place on the focus center before you begin the gathering. Do not wait until it is time to use the water to retrieve it from the refrigerator. This disrupts the flow of the gathering. Do not use plain tap water. This is a special moment that calls for special water.)*

- suggested music *(See "Heartbeat" suggestions on pages 84–85, 91–92, 94.)*

Gathering 5
- small candles, one for each woman *(These may be three- to four-inch candles. The candles must sit securely on the table.)*
- suggested music *(See "Heartbeat" suggestions on pages 96–97, 103, 105.)*

Gathering 6
- feathers, one for each woman *(Bags of feathers of various colors are available in craft stores and/or the craft department of your local discount store.)*
- suggested music *(See "Heartbeat" suggestions on pages 107–08, 110.)*

Gathering 7
- scissors
- prayer beads *(Attractive beads made from a variety of materials, all with a hole cut through the center, are available in craft stores and/or the craft department of your local discount store. The number of beads you need will depend upon the size of your group. If in a large group, provide one bead for each woman. If in a small group, you may provide enough beads so that each woman may choose one bead to represent each woman in the group.)*
- cord of silken material *(Allow 2 1/2 feet for each woman participating. Tie a knot in the cord every 2 1/2 feet. Do not cut the cord into sections ahead of time. This will be done as part of a prayer ritual. The Guidebook instructions for Gathering 7 will tell you how to proceed.)*
- suggested music *(See "Heartbeat" suggestions on pages 116–17, 123.)*

Gathering 8
- stick-on labels, one for each woman *(On each label, print one name from those found on pages 68–69 in From the Heart Journal: A Personal Prayer Journal for Women, along with the name's origin and meaning.)*
- small gift bag to hold the labels
- envelope #1 *(Choose an attractive envelope or decorate a white envelope as you like. Write "Envelope #1" on the outside. Prepare a small sheet of paper for each woman. On each sheet write the*

verses from Psalm 30 found on page 73 in From the Heart Journal: A Personal Prayer Journal for Women. *Fold each sheet, insert them into the envelope, and seal it.)*
- confetti glitter or paper confetti in baggies, one for each woman
- suggested music *(See "Heartbeat" suggestions on pages 125–27, 132.)*

Gathering 9
- ball of yarn
- suggested music *(See "Heartbeat" suggestions on pages 136, 141, 144–45.)*

Gathering 10
- envelope #2 *(Choose an attractive envelope or decorate a white envelope as you like. Write "Envelope #2" on the outside. Cut a small strip of paper for each woman, and write the message found page 85 in* From the Heart Journal: A Personal Prayer Journal for Women *on each strip. Insert the papers into the envelope, and seal it.)*
- suggested music *(See "Heartbeat" suggestions on pages 146–47.)*

Gathering 11
- three candles, one each of yellow, blue, and red
- cloth napkin and bread or matzoh
- envelope #3 *(Use an 8 1/2" x 10" white envelope and decorate it as you like. Write "Envelope #3" on the outside.)*
- small pocket mirror with heart painted on it, one for each woman *(Insert mirrors into envelope #3 and seal the envelope.),* copies of "Participant's Comment Form," one for each woman *(See pages 198–99.)*
- suggested music (See "Heartbeat" suggestions on pages 157–58, 165.)

Gathering 12
- archway made of colorful ribbons *(Use a heavy plastic-covered wire "rope," four feet long. Or, in a pinch, use wire coat hangers. Make the archway ahead of time by entwining long, colorful ribbons around the wire. Allow excess ribbon to hang from the two ends.)*
- heart necklaces, one for each woman *(You can make these yourself by using thin black ribbon and decorative hearts with a hole cut through the top for threading—available in craft stores or the craft department of your local discount store.)*
- suggested music *(See "Heartbeat" suggestions on pages 167, 176–77.)*

Reproducible Handouts
for Introductory Session

Heart to Heart
Overview

Heart to Heart is a time for you

- to come together with other women, relax, and share your stories;
- to sort out your life;
- to reassess God's will for your life.

Each gathering includes
- prayer exercises or rituals to nourish your soul;
- Scripture to enliven your daily life;
- thoughts to help you see more clearly who you are and where you are going.

You will go away with
- friends who support but do not meddle;
- a deeper experience of God;
- down-to-earth practices that will enable you to see the spiritual in the everyday things and routines of your life.

Be-Attitudes

Begin and end on time. Thirty-minute gatherings should end in thirty minutes. Sixty-minute gatherings should end in sixty minutes.

Be trustworthy. Respect each woman's thoughts, feelings, and beliefs, which are based on her life experiences and knowledge. Trust that others will respect you.

Be accepting of each person as she comes to the gathering. Live non-judgmentally.

Be an attentive listener. Do not interrupt when another woman is speaking. Do not talk or whisper to your neighbor when someone in the group is sharing.

Be a supportive and affirming presence. Do not preach, give uninvited advice, try to problem-solve, or "rescue" others. As she gains clarity, each woman will learn to solve her own problems.

Be gentle-hearted with yourself and others. Give yourself permission to share or not to share. Take on the leadership role as the opportunity comes to you—or not.

Be open to share from your true self. Use first-person language—I, me, myself—when speaking.

Be committed to creating a community of the Spirit. Remain focused on your core purpose of spiritual growth. Continually ask the hard questions that will keep each of you centered on your relationship with God.

Be a consensus builder. Make group decisions collectively. Decide together by "weighing in" on the matter at hand. There is no vote. Talk things over, and eventually you will pull together.

Be comfortable with silences.

Opening Hearts
Sacred Story Bible Study:
Great Is Your Faith!
(Introductory Session)

The facilitator reads the following aloud.

Today we will be sampling the Opening Hearts method, one of four Sacred Story Bible Study methods used throughout *Heart to Heart*. Using this method, we will read the biblical text, write our thoughts on a sample journal page, and listen to one another's reflections. In this way we will search our hearts and discern what God is saying to each of us. Remember, this approach is not like a discussion group. Instead, this method of Bible study emphasizes listening and reflecting on the Scripture.

I will read the step-by-step directions aloud one time (omitting the Sacred Story) before we begin. Then I will reread each step, pausing as indicated so that we may work through the process together. We will take turns reading the Sacred Story aloud as indicated. It is crucial that the person reading do so s-l-o-w-l-y much slower than one normally would read—so that what is being read may be absorbed and comprehended.

Step 1: Read. One woman reads aloud the Sacred Story. Remember to read slowly. (two to three minutes)

Jesus left that place and went away to the district of Tyre and Sidon. Just then a Canaanite woman from that region came out and started shouting, "Have mercy on me, Lord, Son of David; my daughter is tormented by a demon." But he did not answer her at all. And his disciples came and urged him, saying, "Send her away, for she keeps shouting after us." He answered, "I was sent only to the lost sheep of the house of Israel." But she came and knelt before him, saying, "Lord, help me." He answered, "It is not fair to take the children's food and throw it to the dogs." She said, "Yes, Lord, yet even the dogs eat the crumbs that fall from their masters' table." Then Jesus answered her, "Woman, great is your faith! Let it be done for you as you wish." And her daughter was healed instantly. (Matthew 15:21-28)

Step 2: Write. As you reflect on the story, write your responses to these questions (one sentence each): What do I see? What do I hear? What do I feel? Pause for two minutes to reflect. Respond as your heart leads you. Your response is unique to you and may differ from others. (two minutes)

I see . . .

I hear . . .

I feel . . .

Step 3: Talk. Briefly share your response. Don't explain. Listen and do not comment on what others say. Receive each woman's offering as a gift. If you don't want to share at any time, simply say "Pass" when it is your turn (four to five minutes)

Step 4: Read. Close your eyes and listen as a different woman slowly reads the Sacred Story aloud a second time.

Step 5: Write. How does the Sacred Story and what others have shared touch your heart? Pause for two minutes to reflect and write one or two sentences in the space provided on page 190. (two minutes)

How does this story, and what others have shared, touch my heart? My heart is touched . . .

Step 6: Talk. Briefly read your responses. Others are not to comment on what you share. They are to serve as Christ's presence by listening and receiving until it is their turn. (three to four minutes)

Step 7: Read. A different woman reads the Sacred Story aloud a third time. (two to three minutes)

Step 8: Write. As your heart is touched by all that you have heard, seen, and felt, how can you now describe God's wish for your life? How is God inviting you to live differently? Pause for two minutes to write one or two brief sentences in the space provided. (two minutes)

What is God's wish for my life, and how is God inviting me to live differently?

   God's wish for my life is . . .

   God invites me to . . .

Step 9: Talk. Share your reflections using "I" statements. Using "I" cares for the mote in your own eye, leaving the splinter in the other person's eye to God's care. You may wish to write a word or two as the person on your right is speaking so that you can pray for her in the next step. (four to five minutes)

Step 10: Pray. One at a time, pray aloud for the woman on your right. Say the person's name and a brief prayer focused on what she shared. The group may wish to join hands. (three to five minutes)

This concludes our formal Introductory Session. When you are through, you may talk quietly until all the groups finish. If you have any questions, the facilitator will be happy to answer them.

Heart to Heart Nametags

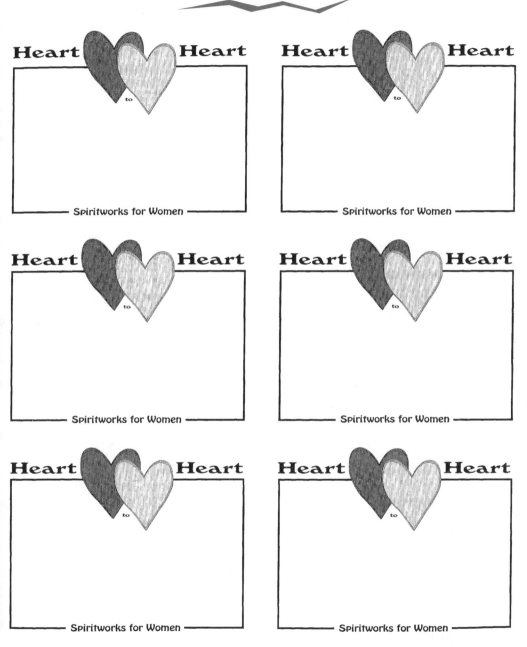

Heart **to** Heart
Spiritworks for Women

Heart **to** Heart
Spiritworks for Women

Heart **to** Heart
Spiritworks for Women

Heart **to** Heart
Spiritworks for Women

Heart **to** Heart
Spiritworks for Women

Heart **to** Heart
Spiritworks for Women

Registration Card

Complete at the Introductory Session or your first gathering.

Name: _____

Nickname:_____

Address:_____

_____

Phone number(s) _____

_____

Fax:_____

E-mail: _____

When is the best day and time to reach you? _____

Would you prefer to meet monthly? weekly? other (specify)?

The best days and times for you to attend a *Heart to Heart* gathering are:

Do you need childcare?

List the names and ages of your child(ren):

What other needs should we be aware of?

Attendance Card

Arrive a few minutes before the starting time. At each gathering, you are responsible for marking your attendance card. Then return it to the envelope.

Gathering #1 _____

Gathering #2 _____

Gathering #3 _____

Gathering #4 _____

Gathering #5 _____

Gathering #6 _____

Gathering #7 _____

Gathering #8 _____

Gathering #9 _____

Gathering #10 _____

Gathering #11_____

Gathering #12 _____

NOTE: Duplicate this page on the front and back of card stock and cut apart, so that each participant will have a registration card on one side and an attendance card on the other. Make enough copies for your *Heart to Heart* group.

Publicity Resources

> *When this announcement is made, staff a display table with a person who is able to answer questions and register women after the service.*

"Good morning. I am *(your name)*. I have been a member of this congregation for *(number of years)*.

"I want to tell you about a new spiritual growth group for women we are starting here at *(name of congregation)*. It is called *Heart to Heart Guidebook: A Spiritual Journey for Women*.

"As you may have read in *(bulletin or newsletter)*, *Heart to Heart* is a twelve-session program in which women come together to pray, study Sacred Stories *(hold up the Bible)*, and share concerns that affect our lives.

"There are three heart-stirring things about *Heart to Heart* that I especially look forward to.

"First *(hold up one finger)*, I'll have a chance to talk with other women about the stresses and strains of being a woman. Some of us take care of kids, a home, and work. Still others go to school full-time or part-time. We may be single, married, widowed, or divorced. This program invites women at all stages of life to meet in a relaxed, comfortable way.

"Second *(hold up two fingers)*, I'll have the opportunity to step back and take a long look at what I'm doing with the precious little time I do have and begin to make decisions about how I really want to live.

"Third *(hold up three fingers)*, I will be able to be me, learn about myself, and grow spiritually. I will discover how being me can be a special ministry to others.

"With *(name of committee chair, sponsoring group, or pastor)*, we are holding an introductory session on *(day and date)*, from *(start time to end time)*. We will meet in the *(location of building and room)*. I invite you to register for this introductory session after worship; a table is located *(location of table)*. We need you to register so that we may plan for the number who will be coming. You also may bring a friend with you; you may register her today or call the number in the bulletin before *(day and date)*. Childcare will be provided.

"Please pray that this new ministry will grow and bless our entire church. There is more information at the registration table. We hope you'll decide to be a part of *Heart to Heart*."

SAMPLE LETTER OF INVITATION

Send this sample letter to prospective participants. Adapt it to fit your particular situation.

(Date)

Dear *(Name)*,

Do you feel your life has become too hectic? If you are like me, you need to remind yourself to

stop,
    look around,
        and remember that this is the "good stuff."

To help you do just that, I invite you to become part of an exciting new spiritual growth group for women. It is called *Heart to Heart: A Spiritual Journey for Women. Heart to Heart* is a twelve-session program that will bring you together with other women to pray, read Sacred Stories, and share concerns that affect your life. There are three excellent reasons to take time now to attend *Heart to Heart.*

First, let's face it: It's hard being a woman. Some of us take care of kids, a home, and work. Others go to school full-time or part-time. We may be single, married, widowed, or divorced. This program is designed so that *all* of us—regardless of our age or stage in life—may meet in a relaxed, comfortable way to look together at our stress factors and our joys.

Second, Heart to Heart gives you the chance to step back and take a long look at what you are doing with the precious little time you do have. You'll get a chance to make decisions about how you really want to live your life.

Third, you'll be able to be yourself, to learn about yourself, and to grow spiritually. You'll discover how being you is a real blessing to others.

An introductory meeting is being held on *(day and date)*from *(start time to end time).* We will meet in the *(location of building and room).*

If possible, please contact *(name or names) (see below)* so that *(she/they)* may plan for the approximate number attending. If you don't get a chance to call, come anyway—and bring a friend or neighbor. Childcare will be provided.

Don't say you can't possibly do one more thing. *Heart to Heart* may be one of the most important things you can do for yourself and for your spiritual health. We hope you'll come.

Blessings,

(name and signature)

Contact Information:
(name or names of planners)   *(phone, fax, e-mail, or whatever)*

SAMPLE ANNOUNCEMENT FOR BULLETINS AND NEWSLETTERS

Heart to Heart
A Spiritual Journey for Women

Heart to Heart is a twelve-session program in which you come together with other women in a relaxed way to share your stories, sort out your lives, and reassess God's will for you. Each meeting contains prayer exercises or rituals that touch the soul, Scriptures that enliven daily life, and thoughts that help you see more clearly who you are and where you are going. You will go away with friends who support but do not meddle, a deeper experience of God, and down-to-earth practices that will help to deepen your spiritual awareness in the everyday routines of your life.

Come to the introductory meeting on *(day and date)* from *(start time to end time)*. We will meet in the (location of building and room). If you get a chance, please contact *(name or names)* (see below) so that *(she/they)* may plan for the approximate number attending. If you don't get a chance to call, come anyway—and bring a friend or neighbor. Childcare will be provided.

Contact Information:
(name or names of planners)   *(phone, fax, e-mail, or whatever)*

Participant's Comment Form

This evaluation of your *Heart to Heart* experience is important. It will help us decide if we should continue to gather in *Heart to Heart* groups as well as offer *Heart to Heart* in the future. Please return it at the end of Gathering 12.

Rate each aspect of the experience:
4–Superb   3–Very good   2–So-so   1–Not for me   0–Does not apply

___ Prayer exercises/rituals
___ Focus center
___ Friendship and support
___ Journaling exercises
___ Relaxation breathing
___ Materials used (feathers, blessing cup, hearts, etc.)
___ Prayers and poems
___ "The Quest of the Woman in Search of Her Heart"
___ Sacred Story Bible Study
___ Music

Please complete the following:

The most helpful aspect for me was...

If I could change one thing, it would be...

Did this experience affect your spiritual life?
If so, how? If not, why not?

Did this experience affect your personal or work life?
If so, how? If not, why not?

Would you like to continue meeting in a *Heart to Heart* group?
Circle one: Yes   No

Name: _____   Date: _____

Address: _____   Phone: _____

Bibliography
of Suggested Music

Inspirational music provides a soulful gateway to spiritual feelings and ideas. Its impact is immediate and nonverbal—and more directly absorbed than complex systems of belief. The power of music is a gift from above that brings together the sacred and the sensual. It connects the earthly and divine. Music carries us beyond the everyday to embody something greater than ourselves.

During *Heart to Heart*, there will be times when you will use music to beckon your group to sit in quiet reflection. At other times, sing-along music will be called for, serving as a special way for the circle to express feelings and beliefs. Other circle rituals will call for music that invites stirring, energized movement.

Don't be afraid to be creative in your selections of music. Music from Greek Byzantine chants, France's Taize, Irish melodies, Trappist monks, American spirituals, and Spanish medieval cantigas are all rich, sacred resources available to you. If you like, go multicultural with all its variety and indulge in Jewish songs, Tibetan chanting and drumming, and West African ceremonial dance rhythms. Whatever style of music you decide to use at various times during your gatherings, it will carry you to symbolic realms that elude your grasp in any other way. Remember, the music is not an end in itself but a vehicle for the renewal of hearts in worship to God.

Call me traditional (my tradition), but I enjoy the more sublime. Here are some of my picks in three categories: "Meditative," "Music for Movement," and "Sing-along."

Meditative

During your circle gatherings, use soothing meditative background music as a respite from the hectic pace of ordinary life. Gentle music playing in the background makes people feel "at home," helps women ease into silences, and covers up disturbing sounds. When choosing music for times of silent reflection, stay away from familiar songs that might distract participants' thoughts during times of meditation.

BoneCroneDrone, Sheila Chandra. Beautiful music for moments of inspiration and insight. You'll appreciate the multicultural pieces.

Hildegard Von Bingen (1098-1179), Anonymous 4. You'll be enchanted by Hildegard's miraculous, mystical music as chanted and performed by the Anonymous 4.

Migration, Peter Kater and Carlos Nakai. Great for prayer and mediation. With selections such as "Initiation," "Surrender," and "Transformation," this music will lead you to recognize the sacred in your life.

Shepherd Moon, Enya. Relaxing, with a Celtic twist. Any of Enya's CDs are great, but this one is my favorite. She is a woman who, by mixing her music in a recording studio, does it all!

Songs and Prayers from Taize, the French Christian youth movement. The music and the accompanying book are both beautifully done. You'll fall in love with their chants of praise. Sing along with the tranquil, repeated refrains.

Music for Movement

Upbeat music may be just the thing your group needs from time to time. Beat drums and shake tamborines, dance around the room, or clap and sway in your seats. Whatever you do, have fun with these feisty, moving songs. Choose a song that goes with the topic at hand, or simply one that will get everyone in the swing for what is to come.

The Book of Secrets, Loreena McKennitt. Soothing Celtic music for the soul. Though this is my personal favorite, anything she has recorded is wonderful.

New Beginnings, Tracy Chapman. "I'm Ready" and "New Beginning" are both jazzy selections that hit me where I live.

A Place in the World, Mary Chapin Carpenter. Whether or not you are a country music lover, you'll appreciate her powerful lyrics.

Walela, Rita Coolidge, Laura Satterfield, Pricilla Coolidge. This sassy recording brings a modern accent to Southwestern music. You'll love dancing around the living room to "Wash Your Spirit Clean."

Sing-along

Hymns, both modern and ancient, deserve consideration when choosing sing-along music for your gathering. All of these selections may be found in *The United Methodist Hymnal* (Nashville: The United Methodist Publishing House, copyright 1989). They also may be found in other hymnals.

Be Still My Soul, Katharina von Schegel. This hymn, written in 1752, is my long-time, all-time favorite. It speaks of God wanting the very best for us.

I Want to Walk as a Child of Light, Kathleen Thomerson. This hymn, written in 1966, is my any-time favorite. It has such a delightful melody and words that will shine in your heart long after the song is through.

The First One Ever, Linda Wilberger Egan. This contemporary hymn, written in 1980, brings to life Maid Mary, the Samaritan woman, and Mary, Joanna, and Magdalene as the first to recognize the Christ in Jesus.

The Gift of Love, Hal Hopson. The words of this hymn are drawn from the thirteenth chapter of Paul's letter to the people living in Corinth. Known as the "Love Chapter," you can wrap your heart around these words. You'll recognize the traditional English melody.

Thy Word Is a Lamp, Amy Grant. This contemporary hymn written in 1984 is popular among all ages.

When Jesus the Healer Passed Through Galilee, Peter D. Smith. Written in 1979, this hymn speaks of the raising of Jarius's daughter as well as Jesus' healing of the bent over woman. You'll want to sing it the way it was designed, with a "Leader" singing the verses and "All" chiming in on the refrain, "Heal us, heal us today!"

Woman in the Night, Brian Wren. Written in 1982, this hymn brings to music six stories of women in the Bible. The refrain invites us to "come and join the song, women, children, men; Jesus makes us free to live again!"

Other sing-along songs to consider are

Her Wings Unfurled; Crying of Ramah; or any of Colleen Fulmer's CD's are at the top of my list. These are a must-have for women's Christian spirituality circles, especially if you like to sing. You may call Heartbeats, 1-800-808-1991, to order her tapes, CD's, and accompanying books.

We Are Sisters: Songs to Support Women's Spirituality and Empowerment, Linda Haydock, snjm, Kathy McFaul, and the Women of Weavers. Intercommunity Peace and Justice Center, Seattle, 1-206-223-1138. Seventeen original recordings used with the *We Are Sisters* ritual book.

Bibliography
of Recommended Resources

Other Resources That Give Guidance

This listing of other resources is neither exhaustive nor complete. It represents only a fraction of what is out there in the arena of women's spirituality. Do as I do and periodically cruise the shelves of a good women's bookstore, or check out the religious or women's studies sections of your favorite bookstore (as you sip your favorite coffee). Occasionally you'll find something in the self-help category, too. Call or e-mail your friends and ask them what they are using. I call it "sixth sense research," and it is my main way of finding new resources.

Altars Made Easy: A Complete Guide to Creating Your Own Sacred Space, Peg Streep. San Francisco: HarperSanFrancisco, 1997. ISBN 0062514903. This book will help release your creativity for your focus center.

Keep Simple Ceremonies, Diane Eiker and (no first name given) Sapphire, Editors. Portland, Maine: Astarte Shell Press, 1995. ISBN 1885349025. Contains practical ideas and fully developed examples of prayer rituals you may adapt to use in your gatherings.

Ritualizing Women, Leslie A. Northup. Cleveland, Ohio: The Pilgrim Press, 1997. ISBN 082981213. Provides a summary of the current thinking about what is distinctive in women's ritualizing.

We Are Sisters: Prayer and Ritual for Women's Spirituality and Empowerment, Linda Haydock, snjm, Kathy McFaul, and the Women of Weavers. Intercommunity Peace and Justice Center, Seattle, 1-206-223-1138. A superb Christian collection of resources.

Women Included: A Book of Service and Prayers, the St. Hilda Community. SPCK, Holy Trinity Church, Marylebone Road, London NW1 4DU, 1991. This book is an inspiring and practical resource for all who share the vision of a fully inclusive Christianity.

Women's Spirituality Web

There are fascinating spirituality sites to explore on the Internet, but I had to really search for the few attuned to women of the Christian tradition. Changes occur on the Web daily, so check it out for yourself. There are all sorts of intriguing pages to explore. For starters:

- **www.LadySlipper.org**—This is a terrific site to check out for music, all recorded by women.
- **www.gracecom.org**—Link yourself into a circle of inspiration through the labyrinth of Lauren Artress and the Veriditas staff of Grace Cathedral, San Francisco. The worldwide labyrinth movement offers women a recovered way (thirteenth century) to connect with God through this walking prayer.

- **www.spiritworks.org**—To talk directly with me about questions you have as you begin your spirituality circle, to read a weekly affirmation, or to attend an event where I'm facilitating, check out the Spiritworks page and send me a message. I'd love to meet you!

Other Resources
by Patricia D. Brown

Learning to Lead from Your Spiritual Center
In addition to management and administration skills, leadership is a spiritual quest. This new model leads readers through five affirmations, or Spiritworks, to enhance spiritual leadership. From the importance of relationships to spiritual survival in a corporate work place, there is no better handbook. Abingdon Press, 1996. (ISBN # 0687006120. $9.00)

Meditations for HIV and AIDS Ministries
Meditations for HIV and AIDS Ministries was written by and about people who have been affected by HIV/AIDS. And we have all been affected. Not one of us will ever be the same since this global health crisis has become a reality. Through the sharing of life stories, this book offers spiritual support that is consoling and hopeful. General Board of Global Ministries, 1993. (Stock # 1838. $2.50)

SpiritGifts: One Spirit, Many Gifts
Is your faith community ready to cease doing what hasn't and doesn't work? Are you ready to stop trying to function like a business and begin to be the community of Christ you are intended to be? SpiritGifts is a dynamic group experience that builds community as participants share together in reflective exercises, discussion, worship, prayer, music, and Bible study. SpiritGifts equips persons for ministries that fit their gifts. Abingdon Press, 1996. (Leader's Resource: ISBN # 0687008573. $19.95; Participant's Workbook: ISBN # 0687008581. $5.95)

365 Affirmations for Hopeful Living
This book is an excellent source of supplementary daily reading for those taking part in *Heart to Heart* gatherings. Acknowledging that

there is no substitute for the power of the Spirit, the author invites you to discover the Spirit's healing presence in your life through daily meditations. Topics include relationships, courage, trust, self-acceptance, and more. Dimensions for Living, 1992. (ISBN # 0687418895. $10.00)

365 Meditations for Mothers of Young Children

Patricia Brown joins eleven other women writers who provide one month's worth each of spiritual reflections on the joys and trials of being a mother of small children. Dimensions for Living, 1993. (ISBN # 0687418909. $12.00)

Worship Resources for HIV and AIDS Ministries

This worship resource will help your local congregation join in support of persons with HIV and AIDS. These persons are part of our communities and churches. Increasingly, we suffer the pain and loss of loved ones. General Board of Global Ministries, 1991. (Stock # 1683 [English], Stock # 1828 [Spanish]. $2.50)